CHRONICLES OF A PARSON'S WIFE
1883-1920

by
Anna Elizabeth Abbott Peck

with
Alice Marion Peck Snow

Edited By
Elizabeth Snow Rowe

Whirlybird Press
Shawnee, Kansas

Cover design by Tim Barnhart
Book design by Judy Ray

ISBN: 978-0-9972541-8-1

First edition
Printed in the United States of America

Whirlybird Press
22052 W. 66th Street * Suite 342 * Shawnee * KS 66226

Rev. Theodore Mount Peck

Rev. Peck with his horse Jenny

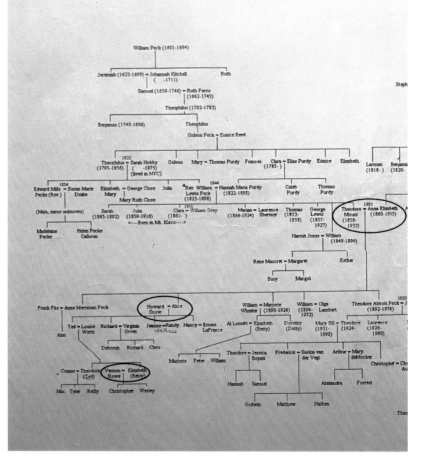

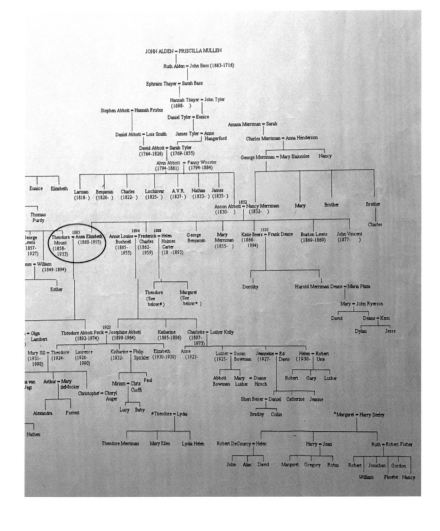

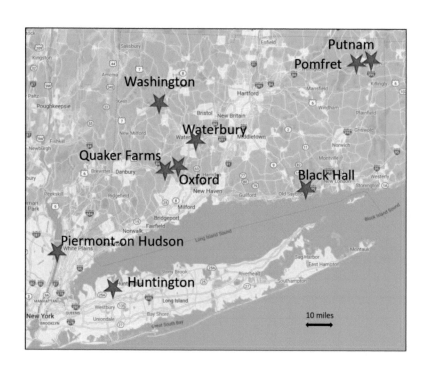

Contents

Foreword

Reverend Theodore Mount Peck, with his bride Anna Elizabeth Abbott Peck, began his career as an itinerant Episcopal minister in Connecticut and eastern New York in 1883. During the first twenty-two years of their marriage, they moved many times. The first eleven years were spent in his first two parishes. Then he served the General Missionary of the New London Archdeaconry, supporting and expanding the Episcopal church throughout rural Connecticut.

During this time, the family grew to include five children. Eventually Theo and his family were settled in a ministry at St. John's Episcopal Church in Washington, Connecticut where he served for fifteen years before retiring due to blindness caused by retinitis pigmentosa. Theo and Anna were my great grandparents, their daughter Alice was my grandmother, and my father Theodore was the third of Alice's four children. My only memory of Anna is of a very old woman sitting in her rocker in the parlor of The Rooftree. That was in the 1950s.

These *Chronicles* were found in one of several dusty boxes of memorabilia that have been handed down through the generations, finally coming to me from the burgeoning attic of my aunt, Nancy Snow LaFrance, Alice's oldest daughter, as she was nearing the end of her life. Those boxes contained many faded photographs and writings, from several generations of Abbotts, Snows and Pecks.

These *Chronicles* were written by Anna Elizabeth Abbott Peck, to tell her children about the missionary days. As she starts out, "Well, my children, you say you want me to write up our family history before I get so old that I lose my memory or my eyes fail me." This remarkable manuscript gives a detailed historical picture of life in the last decades of the nineteenth century, from an intimate personal point of view.

As the family grew, they experienced many of the

tribulations of the times, most of which are strikingly relevant even today. These included brushes with medical care, financial worries, childhood disease, education, finding suitable lodging, and dealing with the weather. The housing and livelihood of ministers, especially itinerant ones like Theo, had the special challenges of being dependent on small and relatively poor congregations. Theo's transportation as he called on his parishioners and provided services at multiple locations was courtesy of a buggy and donated recalcitrant mare. And in the background is Theo's failing eyesight, mentioned only occasionally. In spite of these challenges, the family thrived.

Anna is frank in her opinions about the places and people they meet. The attention to detail, in description and events, and family personalities, is sharp because it is based on her diaries. The *Chronicles* were committed to paper in the form of this manuscript in the 1940s by Anna, with the help of daughter Alice, after Theo's death in 1933, when Anna was living with Alice in the Rooftree, where Anna and Theo had lived since his retirement in 1920.

The parallels of the struggles and achievements of this family, in the face of the challenges they faced over a hundred years ago, with those of today, are striking, and are a testament to the strength of the human spirit.

Elizabeth Snow Rowe

PART I

Early Years:
Marriage and First Parishes

Life in Piermont-on-Hudson: 1883-86

Well, my children, you say you want me to write up our
family history before I get so old that I lose my memory or my
eyes fail me. I thought at first that I would just make it a record
of your father's missionary days, but I remember that when
you were little and I tried to tell you a story, if I omitted the
first part of a familiar tale, you would clamor, "Begin at the
beginning, Mamma," so I think I will go a way back and give
you the highlights of our married life, beginning with the
wedding day.

None of you ever saw the house where I grew up on First
Avenue in Waterbury, a rambling brown house which had
grown with the family of six children. On the twenty-ninth of
August, 1883, there was a great bustle in that same house:
sisters and cousins putting up decorations, helpers in the
kitchen preparing good things to eat, while the slim bride of
twenty-three was in that state of mystical excitement common
to all brides – at least of that day and generation.

I was in my old bedroom, so soon to be deserted, putting
on my wedding finery: new linen underwear – not silk you
notice – the wonderful extravagance of silk stockings, a
borrowed blue garter for the sake of "something borrowed and

something blue," a beautiful petticoat and then the dress.
Sister Mary and Cousin Nellie put the dress over my head,
filmy white silk mull made with a long train and many puffs
behind. Downstairs they fastened the tulle veil with a band of
blush rosebuds – the same veil which has done duty three
times for my daughters. I had a bouquet of blush roses and,
according to remarks when overheard, my complexion
matched them. Perhaps I may be excused at this late date for
telling you that I heard a friend at the reception whisper, "The
prettiest bride I ever saw. I was only a bride once, you know,
and the roses soon faded."

The ceremony was to be at the old Trinity Church, a small
building on Grand Street, at ten-thirty. While waiting for the
time to come, I paraded up and down the long sitting room
with the admiring family looking on. Little brother John, six
years old, having been set on a chair for safety's sake, got so
excited that he put out his foot as I was passing and thrust it
through the end of my veil, making a rent in it.

He was pounced upon by the irate family and put out of the
room and I don't doubt his feelings were much hurt.

The bridegroom arrived from his brother's house where he
had spent the night, arrayed in a new suit bought in some
mysterious manner. I found the record of it not long since in
an old account book, and I think it was bought with money
given or lent him by his father. He looked very elegant.

I wish you could have seen your father at that age. He was
a little taller than I, broad shoulders, short arms which he
swung when he walked, fine head with a roll of curly brown
hair, a brown beard, also curly, a rosy cheerful face, and his
weak eyes improved by glasses.

He was always a great lover, and on this important day
demanded to have me to himself a few minutes before going to
the church. The family party rode downtown in hacks – no
taxis in those days. There were my father and mother, sisters

Mary and Kate, brothers Fred and Ben, small John squeezed in between, Cousins Nellie and Letty. On the Peck side were Father and Mother, sisters Julia and Clara, George Peck and wife.

Our best man was Theo's intimate friend Walter Webb, afterwards Bishop of Milwaukee. The bridesmaid, my only attendant, was Alice Knight, dearest school friend, who now sleeps in France with the boys of the A.E.F.

As we walked up the aisle, I was in the usual dazed state of mind of young brides, but I had been looking forward to it for three years, so was not unprepared. I said my answers out loud, supported by the strong voice of my husband, and I am glad to remember now that the promise "for better or for worse" was never broken. We walked out to the strains of Mendelssohn's Wedding March and returned to the house for a reception and noonday lunch – we would not have thought of calling it a breakfast. Good things to eat were passed around and the men helped.

Then I had to say my farewells, a trying time since I was leaving my home and family for an entirely new and untried life. I was too near tears to linger over it and got around the circle of relatives as fast as possible, gave a last hug to Mother and Father, and escaped through the front gate, where my girlfriends showered me with flower petals and threw a little rice and an old shoe.

We went home with the Peck family to Windsor Locks on the train and stayed there at the rectory a few days to get our breath, then started off on a week's honeymoon. Now take note of this remarkably cheap wedding trip.

We both loved to be on the water, so we planned our excursion accordingly. We took a steamer from Hartford down the river and out to New London, then went out to Eastern Point. In some way that I have forgotten Theodore had heard of a Captain Spicer, a retired sea captain, who kept a cheap boarding house, and had engaged board for us there. We expected someone to meet us at Groton ferry but no one came, so we walked to our hotel – several miles away, sitting on stone walls to rest at times, our bags at our feet. Someone picked us up for the last few miles and we got there before dark.

It was certainly primitive. At the dining table made of long boards we sat with the family and several fishermen and were served with bluefish (their own catch) three times a day. I think your dad got enough fish for once. I know I did, but there were other things too, so Theo got along all right.

Our bedroom was so small that only one of us could dress at a time. The bed was a feather bed, but as the weather turned cool it wasn't bad. We were out for a lark, anyhow, and did not mind inconveniences. The family evidently took great pleasure in inspecting the newly married pair, and we had a good deal of amusement on our part, listening to their "salty" talk and the Captain's sea yarns. There was an organ in the parlor and they asked me to play it. I managed a few pieces and played some hymns for them to sing. There were framed family portraits on the wall, and a big Family Bible on the center table.

Of course what we came for was the sea and we had the beach to ourselves, spending our days there and getting into the water, although it was pretty cold.

I find in the old account book a record of this trip and that we paid four dollars for our four days' stay at the Spicers'. Also I find a record of wedding expenses which makes me smile – the sum total for license, ring, organist, flowers and janitor being just fifteen dollars!

When we left the Spicers' we went to New London and took the boat to Block Island to have a day on the fine beach there. Then we sailed back and took the night boat from New London to New York. By this time we had acquired a good sunburn and I had a very red nose to take to my new parish.

We spent two days in New York with some cousins of the Pecks and went shopping to spend our wedding gold pieces. Cousin Charles advanced some money so we could buy furniture – a dining table and two bedroom sets.

All this time I haven't told you where we were bound for. Your father was the envy of his class at Berkley because he was the only one of them who had a parish engaged before he was ordained. Through the influence of Ed Scudder, college classmate, who had relatives in Piermont-on-Hudson, he was asked to come there and take Christ Church parish as soon as he was ordained deacon.

He went up there in June before our marriage, found a cheap boarding place and looked around for a house in which we could live. There was no rectory and we had to pay our own rent. He found a nice little house with two hawthorn trees in the front yard, and named it Hawthorn Cottage. We could rent it for two hundred dollars a year, and the salary was one thousand. Theo had written me great tales about the beauties of the place, the Palisades rising just behind the house and the quaint Dutch village. Our friends were very enthusiastic about it and thought it just the kind of picturesque place for newlyweds.

Theodore moved his furniture from Middletown and put it in the house. He had only a bed, bookcase, desk and chair. There in Middletown he kept bachelor's hall, even entertaining his brother with wife and baby. I'm sure some of them must have slept on the floor.

He bought a small sailboat and began his adventures, getting upset and sitting on the keel of his boat until he was picked up, starting a reputation immediately as a sporting parson.

So now I was on my way to my new home. When we arrived on Saturday night with our sunburned faces we were met at the station by Mr. Mulligan with a carriage and span of black horses, and taken up the winding drive through the pines to his home on the slope of the Palisades, where there was a most beautiful view of the river. It was called Seven Oaks because of the great trees on the lawn. There were also evergreens all around.

It was a spacious white house with a wide veranda where the family was assembled to meet us. Mrs. Mulligan was a motherly lady about my own mother's age, who made me feel at home very soon. I tried not to be conscious of my red nose as I was introduced to a daughter who was deaf mute and had a very lively young woman as companion.

When we were shown upstairs to our room, we discovered a small round tea table with a large lamp on it marked with our names as a wedding present. I still have the little table, though the upholstery on it wore out long ago. The Mulligans' house was a model of old-fashioned elegance and I thought I was a very fortunate young bride to be made welcome there.

I dreaded Sunday morning when I must appear in church the first time as a bride and rector's wife. I had kept my nose from skinning by the use of cold cream and powder but we both had pretty high color. I put on my light tan-colored nun's veiling with self-embroidered trimming and the little toque that went with it, trimmed with dark red velvet and pompoms. Mrs. Mulligan belonged to the Presbyterian church in Palisades but she left her own service to go with Mr. Mulligan and me so I felt I had a friend with me.

It was a pretty little stone church, nicely furnished and with the choir in a gallery at the back. I tried not to think of the curious eyes looking at me as I listened to my husband preach for the first time and made mental notes of some hints I would give him about his delivery. So soon I began my wifely criticisms – quite shocking! Later I heard a famous preacher say that his wife was his best critic.

After the service I was introduced to the people and was

very cordially welcomed. I don't know what they did after they got home, but I hope I passed my examination. I went home with the Mulligans and felt relieved that ordeal was over.

We stayed at Seven Oaks a week, being driven down to the cottage each morning with a basket of lunch and called for at evening. My "dowry" as Theo called it, arrived in a great packing case from Waterbury and we had great fun building our first nest. No move in later years was so easy and delightful as this.

It was quite a pretty house with a large living room with two bay windows and between them a little conservatory shut off with glass. The only heat was a Baltimore heater with open grate and a register on the floor above. Our friends stocked the small conservatory with plants but they all froze at the first cold snap. Between this room and the big bare kitchen was a small dining room which we could not use in cold weather. There was no bathroom, of course, or running water.

It was before the days of bare floors, and my mother had bought and ordered made a carpet which was fitted to all the bays and jogs by the measures Theodore sent her – a triumph of mathematics (I say). We had heavy curtains across the bays which we could draw at night. Our furniture was scarce, mostly collected from discarded pieces of the Peck and Abbott houses. We had two nice chairs, wedding presents, a round table with cover of olive green embroidered with poppies by my own hands, a very fine "Eastlake" bookcase which Theo made himself while in Middletown, and books to fill it. While in college he used all his prize money to buy books – the English poets and sets of novels, Scott, Kingsley, etc. Then too he had a large case of theological books for his upstairs study. You see we began in a characteristic way; we always had books whatever else we had to go without.

When we had unpacked our wedding presents, pictures and pretty china, it looked refined and homelike. The

Mulligans admired our home and complimented us on our taste.

The back door opened right against a field which led to the Palisades. I wrote my girlfriends that we had a mountain in the back yard. It was clothed with verdure right up to the rocky top, and when I stood in the back door on a bright shiny morning and saw the leaves dancing in the sun, I thought I understood the words of the psalmist, "all the trees of the wood shall rejoice before the Lord."

In our young enthusiasm and care-free attitude we sometimes stepped out on a lovely morning and, leaving unwashed dishes and unwritten sermons, climbed up the mountain hand in hand and squandered precious hours up there, rejoicing in the sun, looking out over the river, and frisking through the woods, oblivious for the time that he was the rector of a parish and I his hard-working wife. Those were happy moments together when our life was so new and the worries and hardships had not begun.

Piermont was a quaint little village. We looked out our front window at a high ridge of rock on top of which the railroad ran. The station was up there and the passengers had to walk down a long flight of steps to the street. Just across the road in front of us the creek ran, salt water from the Hudson. The parson's boat was moored there, so we could start on our excursions at the front door.

On the other side of the creek was a row of little shanties perched up on a rocky ledge. Their backs were towards us and flights of steps led down to the creek. They were inhabited by Irish folk who might have stepped right out of old Erin. The little old women came out on their stoops, in their red petticoats and big ruffled white caps with black poke bonnets over them, their chickens and goats swarming around them, and the goats climbed the cliff above the houses. It was a real old-world scene.

The village ran along by the salt marshes and a long pier stretched out over the meadows to the river. Hence the name – Piermont. There were Dutch and German people in the village, a low standard of living, and much intemperance.

Out on the edge of the river was a fisherman's shack built right over the water which came up through the floor at high tide. A jolly German "fish wife" lived there, just about as broad as she was long. She came to our door every day with her basket of fresh fish, "So cheap," always smiling, her black eyes snapping, a friendly soul. In the shad season the men pulled in a net of big fishes and Theo went down to watch, bringing home a fine shad for a few pennies.

The church was in Sparkill, a higher class village half a mile up the road, where nicer people lived. The upper class people from the Palisades were the main support of the parish. There were also Dutch farmers from the back country as well as poor people from the lower village – quite a mixed parish to manage.

There were calls to make of course and I went with Theo, walking miles over the hills, and always we went hand in hand as soon as we got away from the town. The parishioners might have been surprised to see the minister's wife scrambling over stone walls and running races with the parson. It took me a while to get broken in, but I came to it soon enough.

In this first parish, as in others later on, one of my trials was that I found no companions of my own age, no really enjoyable friends. I always had plenty of kind elderly ladies who were lovely to me and looked after me, and there were ordinary parishioners and poor people to be helped, but no real comrades to have fun with. This made me especially glad to have my sisters and girlfriends visit me. We always had a string of them coming.

We began as we continued, keeping open house for relatives and friends, having a jolly good time and letting the bills go hang – but the first of the month came to be a doleful occasion, when the bills arrived and there was not enough money to pay them.

Here in Piermont it was especially bad because of the pernicious system they had. The salary was small but we could have managed if it had been paid regularly. Not even once a month did the money come in, but only once a quarter. How anyone could live without running up bills, I don't see. The evil habit was started, and having started stayed with us, because we could never catch up enough to start on a cash basis.

Theodore kept strict accounts and I have been amused lately at looking over the account book of those days – discovered in the attic. At the end of the first year there is this record: after enumerating the bills for coal, rent, heat, groceries, etc., he sums up the indebtedness as $221 and the money on hand $44.89, "shortage at end of first year $177!" The salary was nearly that much behind.

The bills pursued us all our lives, but I am happy to say they were all paid before Dad retired and we had the comfort of knowing that we owed no man anything. The Church has now improved its methods, both in larger salaries and more prompt payments.

The vestrymen were so scattered that Theodore did not see much of them. One day he came to me and said, "Nan, I want to invite the vestrymen and their wives to supper."

"Oh, Teddy," I said, "how many are there?"

"Twelve, I guess," he replied.

"Do you dare have little me undertake it?"

"Sure, you can do anything!"

"Well then, all right."

So we went to work to plan our first party. We could not seat them at table so we planned a pass-around supper in the sitting room. I had a girl to help me clean the house and make everything as attractive as possible. We had our pretty wedding china, so that was all right. I made lobster salad, spending a long time beating the mayonnaise. No canned dressings in those days.

I made two cakes and one of them fell, so I had to make another. I was to have hot biscuits and coffee, and for dessert my rich preserved citron with lemon and ginger. A very simple entertainment, but to my unaccustomed hands enough to keep me busy all day. I was tired, flustered, and red in the face when supper time drew near, but finished my work in time to change my dress and powder my face before the guests arrived. I greeted them with dignity and I hope with sufficient cordiality. At any rate my husband's natural exuberance would have made up for my slight natural reserve.

Everything went well. The guests seemed to enjoy themselves and paid me many compliments. Some of the men helped pass the food and there was not the stiffness I had dreaded. I have often wondered what those solemn, bearded Dutchmen and New York Aristocrats thought of the young things trying to entertain them. The Mulligans were pleased anyway, and appreciated the fact that it was quite an effort on our part. When the guests had departed Theodore seized me around the waist and we danced a jig to express our relief and satisfaction with our first party.

In the fall another ordeal awaited me, a visit from Bishop Potter who was to come for confirmation. I had never seen him and had heard a good deal about his dignified personality. Some said he was pompous. We decided not to put on any airs for him. Theo believed that Bishops should see just how their clergy lived. Mr. Mulligan offered to meet him at Sparkill with the carriage, but Theo said no, he would walk up to Piermont station and meet him, so much nearer home. Of course he carried the Bishop's bag.

I had a nice but simple supper waiting – oyster stew, homemade bread, and preserves, coffee and simple dessert. I waited on the table, of course, and sat quietly by while they discussed the business of the parish. As they rose from the table the Bishop turned to me with a fatherly smile and said, "And how does the little girl like it?" Bless his heart, I loved him then and there and he was a good friend to me while we lived there. No one could ever talk to me about Bishop Potter being pompous.

The summer departed and the wintry days began to come on. Theo was very busy, and had started a campaign to do away with the illegal sale of liquor in Piermont village. There was much drunkenness and brawling and he felt he ought to do something about it. He started a law-and-order society, had meetings in the town hall and got the president of the Church Temperance Society to come up and speak.

This kept him away from home a good deal and I began to feel lonely. Also I had intimations that a little stranger was on the way and I had bad feelings and could not take long walks. We were very happy of course at the prospect of a baby, but also felt that it would bring a good deal of financial responsibility. We spent anxious hours with the account book.

There were trying days that winter for the honeymoon glamour was fading and my husband had to leave me alone a good deal. He was working very hard and often came home so tired that he lay down on the couch and went to sleep for the evening. I could not walk up to church Sunday evenings any longer, although I did in the morning. It was pretty lonesome staying by myself and I often got alarmed at noises. Some men in the village were down on the parson for his Temperance work and were hanging around to do him harm. I had a great fright in the night once, when we were sure someone was trying to get in and Theo went downstairs with his pistol while I lay shivering and shaking, expecting every minute to hear a shot. I worked on the baby clothes and dreamed my dreams of him or her and tried not to worry.

Summer came again and brought the visitors. We began the picnics but this time I had to stay home from the rougher excursions. I said to Theo one day, "I feel like my mother, staying home and putting up lunches for the others." Already I had joined the ranks of the self-sacrificing mothers. I did, however, go in the boat to a small picnic place down the river and a few small excursions.

Then late in June it was time for Theodore to be advanced to the priesthood. All this time he had been obliged to exchange with some neighboring clergyman once a month, as he could not administer the Holy Communion while a Deacon. Now the Bishop was to come to Yonkers and have the ordination service there. The baby was due in July and I had no business to go on such a jaunt but could not bear to miss it. I was absolutely innocent as to my looks. I know now, and I often think what a sight I must have been, for there were no maternity clothes in those days, except "Mother Hubbard" wrappers for home wear.

We had to go to Nyack on the train, cross the ferry to Tarrytown and then go by train to Yonkers. We went to the service and after the ordination there was Communion. That afternoon we started home but were too late for the train to Piermont so we stayed with some people in Nyack who had belonged to our parish. I have often thought what a risk I ran, for it was quite a walk from the station and I had such pains that I had to sit down by the wayside to rest several times.

Sisters Clara and Marion came for a visit and Theo took them out on the river one day in his sailboat. Of course they had to have an adventure. The wind died out and Theo lost an oar so he couldn't row and they drifted around until they were picked up by a fisherman's sloop late in the evening and brought to land. It was almost supper time and I had been watching and worrying a long time, knowing my man's propensity for getting into scrapes. I went next door to the

Lutheran minister and asked if I might go up to their cupola to look out. Mrs. Stitt went with me but we could see no sign of the party. She saw how troubled I was and kept me with her until at last they came, very sorry and repentant. My over-strained nerves had to be relieved with a burst of tears.

Mrs. Stitt told Theodore he had better stay off the river until the baby was born and the sailors spread it around town that the parson was out on the river with women, and his wife home in a family way. That did not help the Temperance crusade much.

I had a woman now to help with the work, a Mrs. Pixton who afterward became a steady helper and protégé of our family. She was an English woman, devoted to the Church, was glad to work for a home and five dollars a month. There was also a queer old woman who came in sometimes to do extra work, Mrs. Merman, who reminded me more of Mrs. Gummidge than anyone I ever met. In response to the parson's cheerful greeting, "And how are you today, Mrs. Merman?" she would wring her hands and say, "Very feeble and weakly, thank the Lord, very feeble and weakly."

As my time approached I felt rather forlorn, being so far from my mother and having no especial friend to go to for advice, but we had engaged a relative, wife of a great-uncle, called Aunt Sarah. She was a real natural born nurse who had learned a great deal by being with doctors. There were few trained nurses then outside of hospitals. She was grey-haired, rosy and cheerful, with large strong arms and a motherly bosom such as little babies love. She was to come two weeks before the time to get acquainted with everything, but she had only been there a few days when the baby was born. The doctor sent me no bill, and Aunt Sarah was paid only twenty-four dollars for four weeks, so Nan was a cheap baby, so to speak.

There were expenses enough, however, before we got all her equipment: high chair, carriage, and cradle, though that

last bit of furniture was pretty cheap, as her father bought it –
a swinging cradle – at an auction for one dollar. It was a plain
affair, no beribboned bassinet for Miss Nan, and the whole
family was rocked in it, one by one. It had no rockers, just
swung gently when jogged and many a restless baby went to
sleep after being awakened by a bad dream or some
discomfort, just by a little gentle swing. All wrong of course,
but you all seemed to thrive on it. Rocking the whole family in
a one dollar cradle is quite typical of the way you grew up,
without luxuries.

How I adored the baby, and what a cunning mite she was,
with her wide-open robin eyes and her curly head. I was able to
nurse her and how sweet it was when I had her cuddled in my
arms, her eyes gazing at me as she sucked away.

Aunt Sarah, of course, had not had the modern training,
but was very sensible after all. She kept the baby on regular
nursing hours, and she rocked her, but what baby would not
enjoy that? I enjoyed it too when, in the twilight, I was just
dropping off into a delicious doze and she sat in my room with
Nannie in her arms, singing softly the old German lullaby,
"Sleep, baby, sleep, thy father is watching the sheep." I can still
remember that blissful sensation of rest and peace.

It was very hot upstairs under the tin roof, and Theodore
busied himself in building a nice couch for me to lie on in his
study, which was cooler and had more air. Then when I was
stronger he carried me down stairs for a change. He thought it
was fun to pick me up and go off with me. When Aunt Sarah
had to leave, the grandmothers took turns coming and then the
aunts had to come to see the baby. Of course they all helped
and we had Mrs. Pixton in the kitchen.

It was a very hot summer and the baby cried a good deal.
She was not properly trained but I did not know any better. We
were a very happy little family and felt that the baby made us
quite complete.

We made funny mistakes with her. When she had colic at night we got up and made catnip tea. Theo had a way of holding her against his stomach and squeezing her which was quite effective. I had no baby book or Dr. Holt or child culture, so had to go my own way and learn by experience.

In the fall I had a crushing blow. The owner of Hawthorn Cottage desired to sell it and said we would have to move. So began the long series of getting out of houses I was fond of and taking up my pilgrim staff to move on. I had lived in one house from the time I was born until I married, and it was my nature to put my roots down and stay put, but my fate was to keep me on the move.

Theodore was different. He had grown up in a country clergyman's family and was used to moving. He had adventure in his blood and an optimistic faith in a "rainbow just around the corner." He always thought the next thing would be better while I simply hated to be pulled up and start all over again.

It was hard to leave the cottage, our first little home, just as we were getting fond of it, but it had to be. Theo started looking for a house and finally found one down by the salt meadows with a view of the winding creek and the river with the hills beyond.

I did not see how I could possibly move with the baby on my hands so we decided it was time for me to take a trip home. Theo could leave me there, then come back and move without me. We would go to Windsor Locks to see the Peck grandparents, then to my home in Waterbury. I have thought many times what a fool of a mother I was to take a three-months-old baby on such a jaunt.

As usual we preferred to travel by water, so took the river boat from Nyack to New York and the night boat to New London, or rather Hartford. I sat near the deck in the early evening with the baby wrapped up in my lap and the wind was blowing quite hard. A woman came up to me and said, "Don't you know your baby will get colic in this wind?" She withered me with her scorn and I meekly retired to my stateroom, having dire visions of nocturnal colic with no catnip at hand.

When we arrived at Hartford next morning the boat got stuck in trying to land and we stood nearly an hour in a jam of people trying to get off. Nannie was hungry and she yelled loudly. People looked daggers at her but they had to put up with it. We were jammed in and could not get out of the crowd. Theo put her over his shoulder on her stomach and I tried to smother her cries.

At last we got off and went to one of his Hartford friends to wait until time for the train to Windsor Locks. These people had a baby just Nan's age and when I saw her lying wide awake in the middle of a large bed gazing peacefully around, l realized what I was doing to my poor child and vowed I would never do it again.

One reason for going to Windsor Locks was to have the baby baptized by Grandpa Peck. I was not willing to have it done in Piermont with no family present. This being accomplished we went to Waterbury and exhibited the infant to Grandfather and Grandmother Abbott, aunts and uncles and took her to Watertown to see her Great-grand-mother.

Theo had to go off to do the moving and Aunt Mary Merriman, then young and active, a great pal of mine, offered to see me home and make a visit. I heaved a sigh and started on the last lap of my journey with a great desire to get home and settle down.

We took the boat from New Haven to New York and crossed the ferry to Jersey City. Auntie had to go back to see about the baggage which had gotten left behind, and I sat in the West Shore station and had to nurse the baby regardless of spectators. As I wrote my mother, I blessed her for not crying. If she had, I would have cried too, I felt so forlorn sitting there alone, worried and tired, without a cent in my pocket. I heard the train called but Auntie had not come, so we had to miss it. At last she got there and we took the last train for the night. The poor baby tried to sleep in my lap, but every time a door slammed or a whistle blew she jumped all over and threw up her hands. Theo was in a great state of mind when we got home. He had had his turn at experiencing anxiety.

I wrote my mother: "The house looked so pretty all lighted up, the room in nice order, even the pretty things around looking very homelike. The table was set with the best china and Mrs. Mulligan had sent a lot of flowers and some cake. There was a big plate of luscious grapes and a fine oyster stew in place of the eggs we had expected. Theo had arranged the flowers and everything, and I do think he is a remarkable man to make (these efforts)."

Mrs. Pixton was waiting to cook the oysters and take the baby, so we had our supper in peace. The baby slept all night and most of the next day and I thought she had survived wonderfully well.

Then what did her foolish mother do but take her out on the river in the boat, when Theo wanted to show Aunt Mary everything and insisted that I come too. I held a parasol over the baby's head and she liked the motion, but of course we had to have an adventure. Auntie's hat blew off and in trying to rescue it Theo lost an oar and we went round in circles with the boat rocking on the waves, until after a great effort he recovered the oar and hat. I held the baby tight and prayed that we would not be upset. I registered another vow that I would never take that baby on the river again.

The next event in our lives was the arrival of a horse. Theo had felt the need of one very much, but could not buy one. His cousin Charles Burden in the city was a veterinarian and one of his customers offered him a pet horse if he could find a good home for it. He thought of Theo at once and asked him to come down to inspect the horse. He thought Black Gypsy a beauty, with his glossy coat and long mane and tail and was sure he would be equal to jogging around the parish and country roads.

Theo led the horse to the ferry through the New York streets, brought him on the boat to Nyack, then walked him down to Piermont. There was a barn on the place but of course we would have to buy the hay and oats and have the expense of shoeing etc. Theo managed to borrow a saddle and bridle so that he could ride horseback all around the parish, to his great joy. After several months we got possession of a secondhand top buggy and I could go with him.

We settled down to winter's work. We were so far from church that I could not go very often, and I needed help in the house. Mrs. Pixton had to be with her daughter for a while so Theo went to St. Luke's home in New York and found a woman who had recovered from an operation and wanted a home and almost no wages. Her name was Serena, and she was a curious person with a crooked nose which, according to my brother Fred "looked around the corner." She adored the baby and would sing to her in a deep unmusical voice for hours – "Oh, my baby, oh, my darling," over and over. She went into ecstasies over her – "Oh, this di'mond head, oh, those lovely eyes" – compliments which Nannie accepted calmly.

I could not go to the Sewing Society very often and saw very little of the ladies. We decided that we had better invite them to bring their sewing to our house and stay to supper. I sent out special invitations and prepared a nice supper, set the table and waited. We expected about a dozen, and at the last minute one old maid appeared and no more. We managed to get through the meal at the large table, but had to eat biscuits and cakes for many days afterwards.

This was a serious rebuff and I took it to mean that I was no good as a minister's wife and they did not like me. That did not surprise me, but I did think they might have been more polite. I think the trouble was that we had always lived at a distance from the church and people, while I had been so soon occupied with having a baby that I did not have a chance to get really acquainted. It took some years for me to get over my reticence and inferiority complex.

We were very much worried about finances which got worse and worse. Even the quarterly payments were behind time and not fully paid. We had trouble to get enough cash to pay wages and buy postage stamps. I remember Theo writing to his friend Robert Strange, apologizing for delay in writing because he had not been able to get a stamp and telling about the new house. Robert replied: "What does the pony get to eat while you are waiting for money for a Postage Stamp?" That was the problem, and we had to charge Gypsy's food as well as ours. The trades people were good about it, but we felt ashamed to go on eating and never paying.

Our wedding outfits were wearing out and there wasn't a penny for clothes. I began ripping and turning my dresses, making hats out of odd bits and wearing myself out trying to make a decent appearance.

Finally Theo got desperate and wrote the bishop telling him how things were. He said that the salary was way behind, that we had had a baby and I was obliged to go without things I really needed. He asked if Bishop Potter could secure a stipend from the missionary society of the diocese to help the parish raise the salary. Some contributors had moved away and Mr. Mulligan the treasurer did not know where to look for more money.

The Bishop replied that he would see to it that some help was given and he enclosed his check for one hundred dollars, to be given to me personally with his love. He said nice things about us, and that I had been a heroine (which was news to me!). I was quite overwhelmed by his generosity and wrote a very grateful letter. It was comforting to know that the Bishop liked me if the parish didn't.

Theo said that the money should be entirely in my hands, so I set to work to spend it. Perhaps it was an unholy joy to feel so happy over having money in my hands, but it was like a good meal after starvation just to feel those banknotes and plan what I would do with them. I had the pleasure of paying the most pressing bills, returning a loan made by Father Peck and of buying some new clothes for both of us. I reserved some so that we would not be out of money until the parish could catch up.

Christmas was coming and we planned to celebrate our good fortune by having a turkey. We had no guests coming, so thought we would obey the Scripture injunction and go out in the hedges and highways to get some.

Back of our high board fence was a settlement called the Patch. A door in our fence opened into it and there was a collection of little huts inhabited by Irish and other foreigners. Theo sometimes went through there and looked in on them. He liked to call on one little old woman who seemed to be neglected by her own priest. Her name was Mrs. Grady. Her walls were covered with pictures of the Saints, rosaries and crucifixes, for she was a very devout catholic. She wore a big ruffled cap. Mrs. Grady was very dramatic in her welcome, calling down all the blessings of the saints on the parson's head.

He invited her to Christmas dinner with Mrs. Pixton, Mrs. Merman – the "feeble and weakly one" – Serena and another worker. We tried to get the neglected children of a drunken mother but they were too shy and suspicious to come. The guests had a table to themselves in the kitchen and a fine time, but Mrs. Grady backed out at the last minute, being too timid to risk it. Theo took a plate of dinner to her through the back gate.

We hung up Nannie's little pink stocking, but there was

only room for a rattle and a rubber doll in it. She had some
nice knitted things and new clothes. We had a very happy day
and thought gratefully of the good Bishop who had relieved us
of our worries.

The winter was hard for neither of us felt very well,
perhaps malaria from living so near the marshes. The house
was cold. Nannie had bronchitis in the Christmas holidays, just
as I had planned to go to New York with some of the choir
members to hear the Messiah. I had to give it up and sew
Nannie up in a cotton batting jacket, by the doctor's direction.

While she was sick there was a fire in the village one night,
just across the Patch. I sat in the window watching the sparks
fly in our direction, wondering how soon I would have to rush
the baby out into the cold. Theo joined forces with the butcher,
the baker and all the paddies, pumped the fire engine, carried
water, and finally succeeded in putting out the fire after two
houses had been burned. Ice froze the hydrants and it looked
as if the whole village would go.

Then in the spring another blow fell. Once more our house
had to be sold and we would be on the march again. That
seemed almost too much to me, but Theo cheerfully began
house hunting and found an old Dutch house right on the
street, between Piermont and Sparkill. At least we would be
nearer the church. It was a quaint old place, built against a
terrace so that the second floor opened into the garden, with
stone paths and flower beds. I kept the baby carriage there and
found it quite pleasant except that the railroad ran right
behind the board fence and the noise of trains was annoying.
The front door opened right on the street without even a
porch, which made the passersby seem very near.

As usual we had a romantic house, large and rambling with
great dark cellars which might once have been dungeons. It
was a house that Dickens might have written a story about.
There were rats in the walls and one night a creature ran right

across my face and got into my pillow case. Theo chased it with a poker and killed it. I did not like to be alone in the place, it was so weird.

Here we were when Nan's first birthday came. Mrs. Mulligan invited us to a party at which several one-year-old babies were to be exhibited. She sent Nan a new dress and we went to the party and had a nice time.

We were worried about the baby's nervous condition, and a rich friend sent us some money so that we could have her examined by a specialist. She told us where to go and we made a trip to New York on one of the hottest days of the summer. Foolishly we dragged the poor child around in the heat because I could not miss the chance to shop. I have a picture of her little red face hanging over Theo's shoulder, while he waited for me. We found the hospital after quite a search, but the specialist was on vacation. A doctor examined the baby but could find nothing wrong with her.

We did her more harm than good taking her to New York. We even tried to get her picture taken, but the heat cracked the plate. It was a wonder her brain was not cracked. We got cooled off on the boat and I was glad to get home without disaster. I said to myself "When will we ever learn wisdom in taking care of our poor child?"

The parish was very troublesome, the vestry standing in the way of all progress, probably sorry they had called a young man with new ideas. Theo was tired of struggling with them, so he was delighted when he had a call to St. John's Church, Huntington, Long Island.

I thought it a pretty sad record, living in a place two years and moving three times, although that was not our fault. I looked forward with pleasure to a parish with a rectory, in a settled old town, more salary, and a vestry who promised to pay.

As we prepared to leave our first parish I tried to review

our experiences, and decided what it was that made it so difficult and unsatisfactory. I concluded it was the heterogeneous nature of the parish – so many different kinds of people. There were a few city families far from the center who gave liberally and were nice to us, asking us to their houses at intervals. Then there were the businessmen's families of Sparkill, and the farmers outside, the Germans and lower class people of Piermont, who had nothing to do with Sparkill.

We tried to make friends with them, indeed the German baker was one of our intimates and brought us fresh baked rolls and cookies every Saturday. I went to a German christening party there and saw a great jollification with much beer drinking, but that was hardly our kind of society.

There seemed to be no center and we lived far from the church and had to reach out in all directions. Theo had ideas as to what ought to be done, but could get no support, so he was always running up against a stone wall, and felt that his young enthusiasm and real desire to do good work for the Church and people was wasted. He was sorry not to have accomplished more, but felt he really had made some change in the life of Piermont village and done the best he could.

I had made no friends I was sorry to leave except the Mulligans and Tafts who would still be our friends, so I was not averse to setting sail for a new home, although I thought regretfully of Hawthorn cottage and our first good times of married life. I accepted the fact that I had entered upon a life which would require many changes, so I set about packing up once more and tried not to feel unhappy.

Life in Huntington, Long Island 1886-1892

It was in November 1885 that we packed up to move to Huntington. Nannie was sixteen months old and her little sister was already on the way. Nan was well again, quite chubby, and had brown ringlets hanging around her face. She was just beginning to walk and to say a good many words. We thought she was very intelligent and she surely was good natured.

The move was a continuation of our adventurous life in Piermont. The same Ed Scudder who recommended Theo for Piermont was instrumental in getting him to Huntington. The Scudders' summer home was in Northport, the next town to Huntington, and Ed was on the vestry of St. John's Church. He told the vestry that Theodore was the man for them and they gave him the call.

Ed said there was a steamboat running from New York to Huntington Harbor called the Fanny Garner, on which we could travel and take Gypsy and the buggy along with us. He told us which pier the boat sailed from and we drove down from Piermont, having said our farewells to the people, and made our way to the New York dock.

When I looked at the boat I was dismayed. "Why Teddy," I said, "That can't be the boat. Look how small it is. And no deck or cabin. It must be a mistake."

Theo found the Captain and was told it did go to Huntington, but it was only a freight boat. The passenger boat was called Steamer Huntington and had sailed some time ago.

We secretly uttered maledictions on Ed Scudder and wondered what to do. They were stowing Gypsy and the buggy in the hold under strong protest from Gypsy, so it looked as if we would have to go along. The captain was gentlemanly and said if the lady didn't mind sitting in his cabin she could have it to herself. We ought to be in Huntington in the early evening.

I made the best of it and Nannie and I settled where I could sit and watch the loading of the boat. It took an interminable time and I soon made up my mind that we would be pretty late getting to our destination. I did not know the worst, however, until, having set sail, so to speak, we hauled up at City Island and were told that a storm of wind was rising and it would not be safe to cross the sound. I thought the captain could not have much confidence in his boat and my surmise was probably right, for the sequel to this story is that Fanny Gamer blew up on her next trip.

It was suppertime but no supper. We had brought only enough milk for Nan's afternoon lunch and a few crackers. The Papa decided he would go ashore, and round up something to eat. But when he returned all he brought was a bottle of milk from the last milkman on his way home and some stale baking powder biscuits from a bakery, no butter and two hard-boiled eggs. Nan drank her milk from the silver cup we brought with us and we ate the biscuit, but found the eggs were not fresh.

Darkness fell and we had to arrange a sleeping place for the baby. The captain told me to make use of his cot and I put the baby on the far side of it and lay down myself on the outer edge, with a chair to keep me from falling out.

The captain hung a small light over the door but there was not enough light to read so all we could do was lie there, Theo on the floor with his head on our shawl strap, and listen to the shrieking of the wind in the rigging of the ships tied up at the island. Nan was perfectly cheerful all the time, showing what a good traveler she was. She lay on the cot, kicking up her heels and squeaking her rubber doll, Peter, and giggling to herself. She went to sleep after a while but there was no sleep for us – I knew if I dozed off I would fall out of bed.

About midnight the wind went down and the captain decided it would be safe to cross the sound, so with a great groaning and creaking we started off and had a good tossing when we got out to sea. We heard Gypsy down below, stamping and rolling about, and we felt anxious lest something give way and we be tipped into the water. Nan slept peacefully and proved herself a good sailor, even at that early age.

Before light the boat came into Northport Harbor, as the captain said he did not dare go round the point to Huntington Bay. There was a great racket then, unloading freight, inducing Gypsy to get off and be harnessed to the buggy. He was naturally excited by his night of terror and made considerable trouble.

We did not want to start off in the dark as we did not know the way to Huntington, so we waited until daylight. The captain offered us a cup of coffee and we ate the rest of the biscuits. Nan had a little drink of milk and that was all, but she still kept cheerful and hugged her Peter. We got Gypsy untangled and started off in the chill of a cold November morning to find the Paulding farm where we were to be entertained. I had a large grey shawl and we wrapped Nan in it so only her eyes were visible. She looked comical, peering out of her wooly hood.

By inquiring along the road we found the right way and arrived at the Pauldings' about eight o'clock. They had kept a light burning for us all night and could not imagine what had happened to us. They supposed of course we would come on the regular boat and had been on the dock to meet us. They were quite horrified when they heard we had come on the Fanny Garner and thought it a terrible mistake for Mr. Scudder to have mentioned that boat to us – no one was ever supposed to travel on it. As I before remarked, it was the last safe trip for the Garner and we were lucky not to have been on it the next week.

They gave us a royal breakfast of oatmeal with thick cream, fried ham and eggs and delicious coffee. Nannie had oatmeal and toast and soon afterwards a nice warm bath and a long nap. They thought she was a wonderful baby not to have made a fuss. Little Hiram was just her age and beginning to walk, so they toddled around together and were very cunning.

Besides Hiram there were three girls between five and twelve, a nice family. Mrs. Paulding was a bright little black-eyed woman, a cousin of the Mulligans; they were most hospitable. Mr. Paulding had a large farm out there at West Neck, also apple orchards and a cider mill, where he made and bottled for market the most excellent cider. Huntington was a farming community, very different from Piermont, fine, well educated people, all Americans. Hiram Paulding was the son of Admiral Paulding, famous in history, and his mother was still living with two daughters in a big house near the farm. Madame Paulding was a real, old-time lady, still erect and snappy as a soldier's wife should be. She was a great discipli-narian and the young Pauldings had to step quickly when she called. Miss Anna and Miss Emma were whole-souled, kind-hearted women, devoted to the church and ready to give us their help and friendship.

After we got rested they took us down to see our future home, the rectory, on a hill-top close to the church, surrounded by lawns and great trees, a lovely secluded spot some distance from the village center. The church was brown, gothic in style with tall spire, very dignified and pleasing in its setting of maples and evergreens. There were great beds of myrtle growing along the edges of the lawn and at the rear of the church a little graveyard, burial place of the early settlers of the town a hundred years before. From this graveyard we got a glimpse of the harbor below, blue and serene. There were fields on both sides of the property filled with wildflowers and daisies in spring and there was a barn for Gypsy and a chicken house and yard, so the parson could have his beloved hens. He left some behind in Piermont. It was a wonder he didn't insist on bringing them along in the carriage. How they would have cackled on the Fanny Garner!

The house was quite well furnished by the parish, all rooms carpeted and heavy furniture in parlor and dining room provided. There was a fine large study with built in bookcases which the parson hailed with joy, and a large dining room which I could use for a sitting room and nursery between times. The rooms upstairs were very pleasant and there were two beds, so with our own furniture we would be very well off. Of course there was no bathroom – nobody in the country had those yet – and I may as well tell you how my smart husband improvised one after the first year. There was a small room opening from our bedroom and he had a bathtub put in there, as well as a good-sized oil stove. He ran a pipe from the tub to the kitchen sink, and could pump water through that into the tub. That was carried by a pipe to the kettle on the oil stove and when hot was run back into the tub. It was a great contraption and required some concentration when one wanted a bath. He also fixed a drainpipe so the water ran out into the yard below. I never heard what the parish thought of that innovation!

When our household goods arrived by freight and we had unpacked our personal possessions, the house did look so homelike and pleasant; I heaved a great sigh of relief at the thought that here I could stay and not have to move. I quoted to myself the words of the psalmist, "Here will I dwell for I have a delight therein!" and we did stay for several happy years.

The people were very nice and friendly and when Miss Anna told me that they expected nothing of their minister's wife but to take care of her family and keep the rectory pleasant for callers, I felt like shouting "Hurrah!" No Sunday school class, no sewing society, only my social calls to make, and time to devote to my babies without criticism. Alice was on the way and I had to prepare for her advent in May.

I did so enjoy living close to the church. When I could not go to service I could hear the singing and follow it at home. They had a lovely boys' and men's choir and a city organist and choir master who came out on Friday and had rehearsal, that evening, staying at the rectory over Sunday. Mr. Thompson the choir master was a soloist and sang in Oratorios in the city. On special occasions he gave us some beautiful solos. I remember especially the one, "Oh that I knew where I might find Him" and "If with all your heart ye truly seek Me."

They had choral evensong and Mr. Thompson taught Theo to intone the service. He was already familiar with it from Middletown days and soon mastered it. He had a good voice and loved the responsive service. The whole situation was quite idyllic and reminded me of an English parish, Church and rectory so close together and the churchyard so near. It seemed a lovely place to bring up children and I determined to make my home a model one. Ofcourse the ideal was not entirely carried out, but we were really very happy.

Miss Anna and Miss Emma were our guardian angels, driving in from the farm often and always bringing some offering of cream or eggs or freshly baked sponge cake. They told us about everything and how to get on with the peculiar people, as there are always some difficult ones, even in a model parish.

Our first Christmas we were asked out there for dinner and tree. Nan and Hiram took hands and toddled in to the Christmas tree. Miss Anna had made an enormous rag doll for Nan, which she dragged around.

I must describe the Sunday school tree on Christmas Eve, for I have never seen such a magnificent tree anywhere else.

They had a responsive service and then the enormous tree was lighted with real candles. Mr. Paulding, the superintendent, was quite nervous about it and kept a man with a pail of water and sponge on a stick in case of fire. The gifts were on the tree as well as ornaments, and they included a beautiful doll with real hair and shutting eyes for each little girl. I had dressed one of them and Nan was so crazy for it, she begged all the time I was working on it, but it was too nice a doll for a baby to drag around, and I had to put it out of her sight. Then at the tree, much to my surprise, there was a doll marked for her, the coveted "Dolla" she had begged for. She was in bed, of course, and I sat the doll on a chair in the parlor and in the morning told her to go in and see what Santa Claus had brought for her. She paused a moment in astonishment, then with a triumphant cry of "Dolla, Ha! Ha!" she made a rush for the doll and clasped it to her bosom.

I must not linger over the happy years in Huntington, six happy ones, though broken by illness on my part.

I had no trouble with the second baby. Aunt Sarah came again, as smiling and competent as before, and on a beautiful Sunday morning in May when the world was sweet with apple blossoms and bird songs, Theo took his morning walk and Alice arrived, healthy and serene. Her admirers said she looked so pleasant, as if she were smiling, from the first. A quiet happy baby, not nervous like Nan. The proud father wanted to announce the birth in church, but was a little too modest, so he ticked a notice on the church door: "Born this morning a daughter to the rector and his wife." He was a little disappointed that she was not a boy, but welcomed her just the same.

The parishioners came in with congratulations and flowers. I had great bowls of apple blossoms in my room and said the baby should be our May blossom, happy as a bird and sweet as a flower.

She did not look at all like Nan, straight yellow hair and deep blue eyes. Nan was much interested in her and not at all jealous. Mrs. Pixton had been imported to take care of her, so she did not miss me. Later on when the nurse was gone and Nan's crib put back in my room, she was disturbed if the baby cried and would admonish her, "Stop ky'in baby, suck you little fist and go to sleep!"

We decided to name her for Alice Knight and Marion Peck, so they came for her christening and she was named Alice Marion. Nan went to the church with us for the baptism and looked on with interest. Later she told someone, "Nan did go to church and see Papa water dat little baby." I thought she was cute to compare it to the sprinkling of flowers.

Aunt Sarah sometimes went in for the afternoon service and took Nan with her. She seemed much impressed and would kneel down as soon as she got there and open a prayer book. She loved to hear the choir boys sing.

We had a pleasant summer, sitting out in the shady yard and taking drives to the beach. Huntington Bay was very deep, and had a sandy point running out on each side of it. The beach across the end of the bay was good for bathing and some of our city people had cottages there. They allowed us to use their bath houses, so we had a chance to get into the water, which both Theo and I loved. When Nan was two I made her a scarlet bathing suit and Theo would carry her into the water and jump around with her. She wasn't at all afraid and thought it great fun. Of course she loved to paddle and dig sand wells too. Sometimes we rode out to Eaton's Neck where beach plums grew, and had a picnic. The plums made the most delicious jam, and were also very prickly – the bushes, I mean.

We kept our record of having visitors, and also adventures. Theo would take the brothers and sisters down the harbor in a boat and sometimes get caught out at low tide and be very late getting home. That summer Kate and Marion, our young sisters, were with us and Theo got some of his young people to go on a picnic with them. They were told to take a boat and row all the way around to Eaton's Neck, having laid in a load of clams for a bake, while we were to drive there with a large basket of lunch and meet them, bringing the babies also. Then we would have a clam bake and picnic together. Theo and I carried out our part of the contract, got there and amused ourselves on the beach, took turns going in swimming, and waited for the folks with the clams. They did not come and we got hungry and ate our lunch, wondering what they would do with only raw clams. I remember Nan stumbling around in the plum bushes, getting scratched and wailing, "Give Nan buggist (biscuit) and little piece apple-u." Alice slept peacefully in a hammock hung in the bushes, protected with netting, and made no fuss. No party arrived and we had to go home without them and the clam bake. Theo was anxious about the young folks and spent the evening trying to find out where they were. At last they came toiling home when the tide turned, and said they got lost and couldn't find Eaton's Neck and then got caught on a sand bar and had to wait for high tide. They roasted some clams and had nothing else, even water.

We had another funny adventure on Eaton's Neck, when we took a young clergyman from Northport with us to go swimming. He undressed in a thicket of plum bushes and left his clothes there while he went quite a distance down the beach to be sure of privacy as he had no bathing suit. We played around for a long time and then decided it was time to go home. Theo began shouting for Sanford but got no reply. He hunted all over the place, shouting as he went, and began to be alarmed about the young man when he descried a nude figure away down the beach, waving its arms and shouting: "I can't find my clothes!" He had wandered so far that he could not tell which clump of bushes was the right one. Theo joined the search and succeeded in finding the right place and the poor young man was able to dress. We had a good laugh at the young parson.

The next winter Theodore made up his mind to study for a M.A. degree, so bought books and started on a course in philosophy. In the spring he went up to Hartford and received his diploma as Master of Arts. He said he could not afford a hood so never get one. I kick myself now for not insisting that he should have one, even if it meant going without a few meals. He felt he could not afford it, so all the good it did him to have a degree was his extra learning and the privilege of writing M.A. after his name. Every time we went to a scholastic occasion, and I saw the colored hoods worn by young sprouts just out of Divinity School, I felt it just wasn't right but at least I knew he had the learning.

In Huntington he had his first white stole, embroidered by Miss Emma. They had the different colors for the altar and a very lovely service.

For those seven years he had a parish where things were done properly, everything reverent and beautiful, no high or low to fight about, all of one mind as to ecclesiastical detail, and no extremes. His preaching pleased the people and taught them right living. I heard that one woman of the poorer class said, "If you want to hear the real Gospel preached, go to St John's."

There were some things he wanted to change, one being the sale of pews, a custom which had come down from the early days. People liked to sit in the same places and the pews were auctioned off once a year. Theo did not believe in that system. He thought the church should be entirely free, so he worked away at it, till he got the consent of the vestry after considerable opposition, to stop the sale of pews, and adopt the weekly envelope system, asking every member to subscribe to a definite payment. This was carried out and made an improvement in the feeling of the less lucrative members.

People still sat in their favorite places but saw to it that strangers were welcomed.

Another effort in the parish was the starting of a mission to the Harbor. There was quite a settlement of sailors and fishermen's families who would not come up to the church. He got the gift of a disused corn crib and had it made into a little chapel, simply furnished. Someone loaned a parlor organ and every Sunday afternoon some members of the choir and others would go with him to lead the service. It was quite gratefully accepted by the Harbor folk.

Theo also held Services at Huntington Station, several miles from town.

Miss Emma was an enthusiastic church worker, and encouraged and assisted him in all his endeavors. They contrived together to set up a coffee house for men on the main street of the village, to keep the men out of the saloons. It went on very well while we were there.

Miss Emma had a sewing school on Saturdays in the Sunday School room and taught the little girls to sew and make their own clothes. There was also St. Agnes Guild for young women, directed by May Holden, who taught the girls to make the altar linens and do fine embroidery.

While we were there Theo started the first Woman's Auxiliary. The movement had just commenced in New York and Miss Emery, the first great leader, came out and spoke in the church, and the women got together for missionary work. We began the packing of barrels of clothing and Christmas gifts which has always had such a large place in my parish life. I was glad to have them come to the rectory for this and to help in the work.

In summer we were out of doors most of the time and in winter we had cozy times in the house. I had to sew a great deal, making their little clothes without a machine, while they played with their dolls and toys in the dining room. When twilight fell I would put away my work, take the baby on my lap and sing nursery jingles and tell stories, having no prejudice about Mother Goose and the old fairy tales. Sometimes we went into the study and sang songs with the small baby organ, owned by the parish. They learned to sing very young. Alice could carry a tune when only two. Nan already showed her artistic talent and was always drawing and coloring. Her favorite subject was little girls walking in flower gardens, processions of them with birds and butterflies around.

Of course they were brought up on Bible stories from the old "Brown Book," worn to shreds before the family grew up. Nan was so imaginative that she made them a part of herself at once. I was reading the story of the angels at Christmas and she went to the window and looked up at the sky and said, "Nan sees the bright angels," and I don't doubt she pictured them very plainly. She made such funny remarks when she looked at the pictures, she would laugh and giggle at Moses in the bulrushes and say, "Oh, what a cunning little fellow he was!" She got the camels and Ishmaelites mixed in the story of Joseph, and when Alice was going around on all fours with her back humped up, Nan went into fits of laughter and chortled, "Baby's a Mishmalite." I kept a book of her funny sayings and gave it to her some years ago, but it is probably lost by this time.

Theo's eyes were now troubling him a good deal. He could see things straight ahead pretty well but could not see what was under his feet or at one side, so he was always tripping over something or bumping into someone. He could not see the babies on the floor when he was in a hurry and often stepped on them. Nan got so that she would run if she saw him coming and say, "Nam better run, Papa step on me, kill me and die me and put me in a pit, — and.dat be berry wicked." This must have been a reminiscence of Joseph, I suppose. When

she said her prayers she asked God to make Papa a good man
– not to kill little girls. One morning he stepped on her again
and told her she must have forgotten to say her prayers. He
could not see in the evening, so tried not to go out unless
someone came for him.

I used one of the bedrooms as a playroom when they were
a little older and he sometimes came in to see us. I had my
sewing machine then and there was always a heap of things on
the floor. He came in one day, put his foot into a little red cart
and slid all across the room, coming down with a crash in the
midst of the playthings, which set the children into fits of
laughter. He would romp with Alice and tell her she was his
boy and do all kinds of tricks with her. She learned to say when
asked her name, "Alice boy-cape." (She could not quite manage
Peck.)

As she grew older she and Nan were great playmates. Nan
called her baby or Babe and they did all kinds of monkey
shines together. Alice was always a kind of little clown, so full
of fun, and would do tricks on purpose to make Nan laugh.

I've often had supper outdoors on the little round table –
still with us – as they went to bed before the family supper. I
remember one birthday on the lawn – it must have been when
Nan was three – and we were all three decorated with wreaths
of daisies and clover on our heads, sitting around the table
with a tiny birthday cake on it, when a lady parishioner called.
She looked rather surprised to see me so decorated, but I loved
to play with the babies and did not care who saw me. I spent
almost my whole time with them in those happy days as I had
no nurse, but usually managed to keep someone in the kitchen.
I read to them a great deal, all the old favorites, and Nan
learned to read very young. Speaking of her imagination, I was
interested to have her say, when she published her first book,
that the different characters were drawn just as she imagined
them in her childhood, especially that remarkable picture of

"Baa-baa-black sheep" which she says was just the way he looked to her when I first read about him.

When Nan was three and Alice was one-and-one-half, we started our traditional Christmas, which you all remember through the years. We hung the stockings and read "The Night before Christmas" as well as the Bible story, and they came laughing down the stairs in the morning to see the stockings. I also remember that I sat up very late Christmas Eve dressing dollies while Theo worked on his sermon. Then we had a little tree on the parlor table which was lighted and we joined hands and walked around it singing "Gather around the Christmas tree," Papa leading in his jubilant voice. Alice was rather overcome and dizzy I suppose, for she kept saying "Baby lie down," and wanted to stop. You (children) will remember how those customs were kept up throughout the years, and how when old enough, you always went to church on Christmas Day.

It was about this period that we made the remarkable trip to Fire Island. I think some of the venturesomeness of our earlier years must have returned and we wanted to break loose and do something wild. Theo had already made the trip with his brother George, driving across the island and then going by boat to Fire Island across the bay to the narrow strip of surf right on the open ocean. They risked their lives swimming in the surf, with no guards or lifelines, and Theo was "hankering" to do it again, and have me go along. My sister Kate was visiting me and she was ready for adventure. Of course we had to take the babies and be gone all night. Theo had discovered some Abbott cousins living in Babylon and "wangled" an invitation for us to spend the night there. I have thought since that it was a decided imposition.

We started out in a two-seat wagon, baby on my lap and Nan on the back seat with Kate. It was hot and dusty and the mosquitoes in the middle of the island were terrible. The children fretted and scratched and we had to keep our arms waving in self-defense. We got to Babylon and took the steam launch to Fire Island – just a desolate strip of land between the bay and the great devouring ocean. There was a heavy fog so we could not see far off, and the great waves were breaking on the sand. It looked very dangerous to me as there were no lifelines and no one near and the fog obscured the view. Theo went in swimming and I thought I had lost him in the fog and tremendous surf. I held my breath till he came out again. The undertow was terrific and even he was a little frightened. We had our lunch and the babies played on the sand a little, but it was very depressing to me – the feeling of isolation in the fog and the great devouring ocean so near. I was glad to get back to the mainland. Baby cried on the launch going back and was evidently the worse for wear.

We found the cousins, who were very polite, but I felt we were trespassing on their hospitality, as the mother was away and only Will and the little girl and the housekeeper were there. They gave us strawberries and ice cream after supper, which they brought from a church festival. As a consequence there were stomach aches in the night and not much rest.

We started for home right after breakfast, having thanked our host profusely and invited him to return the visit. The children were tired and cross and I felt we were a long way from home. It seemed a much longer trip than when we came over. Baby fretted and Nan insisted on slipping down on the floor and sitting between Aunt Kate's feet. The Auntie tried to cheer her by laughing at her and calling her, "Nanny Goat." She grunted out, "Ain't Nanny Goat – ain't nuffin." It began to drizzle and the mosquitos were so thick on Theo's back that I could hardly see his coat. Baby wailed and we were all very damp and much bitten, and I thought it was decidedly a "pleasure exertion." Serves me right, I said to myself, for taking babies on such a trip. If we had been by ourselves we could have made a lark of it, but there was too much responsibility this way. It seemed as if we would never get home but at last we did, and made a big fire in the study fireplace and stretched ourselves out in front of it to recover. Alice had a sore throat the next day and we had to get the doctor, so the excursion wasn't very profitable. We decided to be satisfied with our home beach and bathing.

When the little girls were old enough they went to church and were pretty good. Alice always insisted on having a hymn book and singing in her own way but nobody minded her little voice. She was training for the choir already.

In the next seat to us were three very handsome children with lovely black eyes. They were with their mother, Mrs. Richard Derby, of New York. Dr. Derby was a noted eye specialist. Our little girls were much interested in the boys and stole many looks at them. They were named Richard and Roger and when they grew up Richard became the husband of Ethel Roosevelt. They were a lovely family with a fine home on Lloyd's Neck and were very good to us. The little girls were released before the sermon and would then go and sit in the church yard under the eaves of a small Negro church, which seemed to have been built under our protection, it was so near. It was just over the fence and our youngsters would sit there and listen to the strange sounds of stamping of feet, clapping of hands, and the singing in loud voices of the same tunes over and over. The girlies were fascinated by it and listened whenever possible.

One Sunday when they came out of church they found the rectory full of smoke and Katie the maid nowhere to be found. They did not know what to do about it so sat on the steps till I came, when they told me they thought perhaps the house was on fire. Smoke was pouring out of the windows so it looked rather that way. I rushed to the kitchen and found a pot of chicken burned to a crisp. I snatched the red-hot kettle off the stove and threw it out the back door and opened the windows. Katie was discovered in her attic room enjoying a novel. We ate baked beans for dinner that Sunday and it was a long time before the house recovered from the smell of burnt chicken. After that when the girlies wanted to tease Katie they would begin chanting, "Katie burned the chick, Katie burned the chick," over and over. Katie got very mad but that was her punishment.

They had no playmates but each other, being so far from the village but they were happy together in spite of some quarrels. Alice was quite willing to let Nan take the lead, as a rule, and she had imagination enough to think up plenty of games and adventures. When the daisies were in blossom in the big field next us, we would go in there and pick great bunches of them. Alice's head was just as high as the daisies and I loved to see her yellow hair shining in the sunlight. She had wavy hair which curled a little on her shoulders, while Nan's was long and curled in ringlets, a lovely chestnut brown. Her eyes were grey and very wide open, her mouth a little inclined to turn down, while Alice's was always upturned, ready to smile. They loved the outdoors, birds and flowers, and were usually pretty good, though not angelic. When Nan was naughty she was put in the closet to repent, and when Alice had a fit of temper and wouldn't mind, she sometimes got a few slaps. The only thing they were really spanked for was disobedience, as for instance when they went down the cellar and played in the coal bin with their clean white aprons on, or when they got into the chickens' drinking water and soaked themselves. A small neighbor, Annie Hall, was their evil genius. I did not like them to play with her, but could not always send her away. One day I had been out for a while and Annie came to see them. When I returned they had taken down the best little coffee cups, which was strictly forbidden and were having a party with them. I knew it was Annie who proposed it and I sent her home, but also felt obliged to administer spankings. One day Nan ran away with Annie and was gone a long time, returning with her new pink dress in tatters from crawling through wire fences. She had to go to bed that time.

While we lived there we had many visitors, the brothers and sisters both sides, and my friend Alice Knight, also my parents, who enjoyed coming to see us. They all loved the place and thought it was fine that we could always live in such interesting regions.

Once my sister Mary and Aunt Mary Merriman came together. We called them Molly and Aunt Polly and when I told Nan they were coming she said, "Nan's afraid of Molly Polly" and ran and hid. She found they were pretty nice when she got acquainted with them. We had excursions on land and water and there was much cooking to be done. We had more money than in Piermont but even so the bills would get ahead of us sometimes. However, we considered the entertaining of our friends our one luxury.

So far we had all been well, no special illnesses to contend with and then in March 1888, just as the great blizzard was beginning, I went to bed threatened with a miscarriage, and that was the beginning of a year's invalidism and a weakness that troubled me the rest of my active life.

I will not go into all the details of that strange and unusual experience. If any of you are interested enough you can read the history of it in the letters I wrote to my mother which I retrieved after her death. Suffice it to say that I was in bed all through the blizzard and the months of May and June, and at intervals through the summer.

The great blizzard must have special mention, having become a historic spot in the history of American climate. It began with freezing rain, then changed to snow and before we knew what was happening we were lost in a blinding storm so thick that we could not see the church or even the hen house.

Theo went out to put the hens up and found some of them roosting in the apple tree, blind and dazed and half frozen. He put them into their house and nearly lost his way getting the few steps back to our house. The storm was blinding and went on for two days. We were cut off from the world, no mail, no trains coming, no provisions brought in – just a white waste of snow.

I needed medicine and we had no meat, so when the storm abated Theo started to walk to the village. The deep valley between us and the village street was filled with snow up to his chest. It was all he could do to get through the drifts. He took a board and pushed it ahead of him as a kind of life preserver. He got to the doctor's house and told him about me.

Doctor Banks said he could not possibly get to me but sent medicine and said I was to stay in bed. Theo secured a beefsteak and a few groceries and struggled back through the drifts, arriving nearly exhausted. We heard of some sad cases, one especially an old couple marooned and sick with pneumonia and found frozen to death.

It was a strange sight when I looked out the window, snow piled up almost to the second story, a great drift in front of the horse shed, so high that little Nan, when let out, walked right up to the roof. The sleet mingled with the snow had frozen it hard. Theo had hard work to break through to the barn and water the horse and chickens. No mail came for a week and then the steamer broke through the ice of the harbor and brought mail from New York. It was hailed with cheers by the populace who turned out to welcome it, and with shrieks from all the boat whistles in the harbor. No trains ran for another week. It was a long time before roads were opened and ordinary life could go on.

I lay in bed all through May, hoping to save the baby I hoped was there, and I remember watching a robin building

her nest near my window and then patiently sitting on her
eggs, waiting for her babies. I thought I was doing the same
thing, hoping to get my baby alive.

The wrong condition went on all summer. I would be up
for a while and then back to bed. This upset the household
arrangements, and we had to get someone to look after the
children. My dear husband was always the best of nurses and
all through my sickness and weakness was so patient and
cheerful and ready to help that we got along with only the maid
in the kitchen, but of course he had his church work to do and
could not always have the children with him. We got a grey-
haired woman named Mrs. Toombs – not a very cheerful name
– but she was good help and the children liked her. I would
hear Alice's little voice piping up, "Missa Toombs!" She could
not stay very long and then we got a girl named Phoebe – the
girlies called her the Phoebe. She played with them and did
very well. My doctor went away for the summer and I had no
advice about my sickness. I did not increase in size very much
and so concluded that the baby would be small and delicate. I
knew afterwards that the parishioners were looking at me and
saying, "She's not going to have a baby."

I prepared a special outfit of Jaeger flannel made with the
Gertrude suit, just coming into use. My time was supposed to
be early in November and I engaged a nurse for that time – not
my dear Aunt Sarah, who had gone out of the nursing
business. I also asked dear Aunt Carrie to come and of course
bring Jean, so the little cousins had their first visit together, so
often to be repeated through the years. They had been given a
great dollhouse which stood in the upper hall and was most
beautifully furnished. It had four rooms and a complete family
of dolls, Papa, Mama, and all. They played with it for hours
and it kept them quiet.

When Dr. Banks returned I told him of my unusual
behavior and he was frankly puzzled but did not suggest seeing

another doctor. I know now that he ought to have sent me to a specialist at once, but he never even made an examination himself – just had faith that it would come out all right, and I, being entirely inexperienced, had faith in him in spite of my worries. If he had examined me as he ought to have done he would have found no signs of life and I would have been saved months of worry and trouble. He was an old fashioned country doctor, but being so near New York I fail to see why he did not keep more in touch with modern medicine.

My mother made me a visit and she always insisted afterwards that she was sure I had had a miscarriage. She did not try to direct me, but since I have been a mother myself I know how she must have longed to take matters into her own hands and bring a competent doctor.

The nurse came, Aunt Carrie was on hand and everything ready. I think both women were suspicious that nothing was going to happen. They were better observers than old doctor Banks.

On the day I expected the baby, hemorrhage came on again. The doctor pulled his beard in perplexity but stuck to it that everything would be right – said that birth sometimes began that way.

I lay there two days longing for a pain with all my heart and strength. Never before had I wished for a pain but it seemed my only hope. It seemed as if I could not endure the suspense another day and I told Theodore he must see the doctor and tell him that something had got to be done. Imagine him leaving me alone all that time. I think he was afraid to come.

Theo went to his house and gave him a strong talking to and said that I was at the end of my patience and would go to pieces if I could not be told what was wrong. The doctor came and made the long deferred examination and of course found no signs of life. He went home and sat up all night with his books and returned next day with the decision that it was all a mistake, there was no baby, only a tumor, which sometimes showed the same symptoms and deceived people: he would send me to a specialist in New York before long.

It was hard to restrain my indignation at him for not finding out sooner, and now I had to face the hard task of swallowing my disappointment and chagrin and letting everyone know I had made a mistake. It was a bitter pill, but I knew I must make the best of it, so as soon as I felt better I got up, dismissed the nurse and let Aunt Carrie go home. I could not bear to face the people and wrote a note to my good Miss Anna, telling her all about it and asking her to tell the others and say I did not want to talk about it. She wrote me a lovely note of sympathy and understanding and I felt a little comforted.

I went out for the first time Christmas Eve and it was about as hard a thing as I ever had to do, to walk into church knowing that everyone was looking at me.

The slow doctor again kept me waiting, much against my will – said he wanted to observe me further before going to New York. I was sick at my stomach every morning, a new development which nobody understood. Looking back at it I wonder we did not take things into our own hands and go to some other doctor, but we had always felt strongly about being loyal to our own physician. So we held on and waited. I had the words "time and patience" said to me so often that I never wanted to hear them again.

At last, the first of February, he got to the point of taking me to New York. I remember I lost my breakfast before starting. Dr. Thomas was the leading specialist at that time and we made our way to his office. He listened to Dr. Banks' hesitating description of my symptoms, and when he asked for a detailed history of the past nine months, Dr. Banks turned to me and said, "She'll tell you." I gave a clear and concise report of exactly what happened, for it was indelibly impressed on my memory.

The great doctor nodded in approval and proceeded with his examination. It took him only a few minutes to decide my case. He said there was no tumor – that there had been a fetus and it had been partly discharged, but the remaining membranes had grown fast, keeping up the appearance of pregnancy, and the organ had gone on enlarging until it was the size of a six months fetus. He said he could set me right by an operation if I would come to his sanitarium on Lexington Ave. and I ought to come as soon as possible. He said there would be no charge for the operation and the board would be, as we understood it, forty dollars a week. I would stay two weeks. He talked with Dr. Banks privately and I hope he told him what he thought of such delay. He told us that if it had gone on much longer, it would have run into hydatidiform tumor – a watery tumor.

After we got home and wrote Dr. Thomas again, we found we had made a mistake about the price. It would be sixty dollars a week and Dr. Thomas said he could make no reduction as he had a partner in the sanitarium, but he would not charge for the operation. He said if we could not afford the price I could go to the Woman's Hospital and he would refer me to a friend of his there, and I could have the same treatment.

I was terribly disappointed for I had fallen in love with Dr. Thomas and did not like the idea of a big hospital. Once more I had to swallow disappointment for it would have taken more than the whole of Theo's monthly salary to pay the bill for two weeks.

My mother had agreed to take Nan and Alice for the two weeks, as Theo would be with me most of the time and we would have to close the house. I worked hard to get their clothes ready. Theo took them across the sound by steamer and then by train to Waterbury. They were much excited at going to Grandma's and chattered constantly, but I felt forlorn, not knowing whether I would ever see them again.

When Theo returned he went with me to New York and we stayed at the Scudders' home until I was admitted to the hospital. The great building seemed to me very depressing. It was my first impression of a hospital and I felt very forlorn when Theo left me. He had to go home for Sunday and I could not see the surgeon I had been assigned to until Saturday as he only came there once a week. I could go out if I got a pass from the office, and I felt like a boarding school girl.

I had to repeat my report to various doctors and go for treatments preparatory to the operation. The patients who were out of bed took their meals in a cheerless dining room and were a depressing sight in their kimonos and sad faces. There was a sign posted, "Do not talk about symptoms at the table," so I escaped that. On looking out of the window I noticed a large building quite close and asked what it was. They told me "the morgue" which did not add to my cheerfulness. I began to get more and more frightened and had a feeling that I would not live through if I stayed there.

On Saturday Dr. Nicoll came and I was taken to the operating amphitheater and put through an examination before a class of students, sitting on tiers of seats with their notebooks. This was a great ordeal and when Dr. Nicoll took me aside and said that he felt very uncertain about my condition and could not operate till he had talked to Dr. Thomas, my heart went down to my boots. He saw that I was distressed and he was very kind, saying the hated words, "time and patience." I asked when I could see him again and he said not till Saturday – a whole week. I felt I could not endure it, and when I saw patients pushed off in corners, lying under ether, I got such a fright and feeling of horror that I knew I would die if I stayed there.

Mrs. Derby sent me some lovely flowers and I managed to survive Sunday by distributing some of them to patients sicker than I and making friendly calls. I also attended a service held for the patients and tried to calm my fears.

When Theodore returned on Monday I fell on his neck and demanded that he take me away from there or I would die under the operation. He was distressed and indignant when I told him I had to be kept waiting another long time and he went right to Dr. Thomas and told him he would have me come to the sanitarium if it took his last cent. Dr. Thomas agreed that it was not right to keep me waiting any longer and said if I would come to the sanitarium that night he would operate the next day. He would make it right with Dr. Nicoll.

Theo went to his friends the Scudders and told them about it and they said it was the only thing to do and they would help with the expenses. Afterwards the Derbys also contributed so it did not cost us much more than to stay at the hospital.

Theo came back and told me to pack my bag and we would leave at once. It proved to be not so easy. I was held up by the house doctor who said I could not leave without a permit from Dr. Nicoll. They telephoned him but he was not at home, so we had to wait, and then the house doctor summoned the Board of the hospital and I had to appear before them and state my exact reasons for leaving without treatment, and give my history for about the sixth time, and to men who were not doctors. This was most trying and I put in a strong plea on the ground that I had left home for only two weeks and must get back to my children. After much discussion they allowed me to withdraw, and gave me permission to leave as soon as I heard from Dr. Nicoll. We waited and waited and every time they sent him a message he was not there. It was getting late and I was tired out and at last Theo got out of patience and said we would go anyway. The house doctor put on his blackest looks and said we would be put on their black books and never allowed there again. That did not trouble me, you may be sure, and Theo told him so quite plainly. The nurses begged me not to go, but we could not wait any longer and "eloped," as they called it, down the corridor, the nurses trying to hold me back and the doctor looking like a thundercloud.

We got to Dr. Thomas's place about nine o'clock and what a haven of rest it did seem to me after all my troubles, such a bright, attractive place, kind nurses, and everything cheerful and comfortable. They left me feeling so relieved and hopeful, and they put me to bed and prepared me for the operation next day. In the morning Theo came and stayed with me till it was time to go to the operating room and I left him without fear. I had time to look at the instruments and queer things before the doctor came in, but I was not at all frightened. Dr. Thomas came in and took my hand and said he wanted to get me through my troubles. I said I was sure he could. It was rather hard taking the ether and I felt as though I were choking to death, but soon went to sleep and knew nothing more until I waked up in my bed and Theo was holding my hand.

What a blessed sense of relief it was to know that my long waiting was over and I was going to get well. My heart went up in true thanksgiving to God and Dr. Thomas for all his goodness to me. My two weeks and more in that happy place made up for a good deal that I had suffered. I had flowers and visitors; my New York friends and others who happened to be in the city came to see me. One very welcome visitor was my dear master, Dr. Russell, now serving in the Divinity School in New York. He wore a long black cape, and with his saintly face and manner seemed something like an angelic visitor. He gave me his blessing when he went away and I don't think I ever saw him again. I had my babies' pictures right by my bed and talked to them every day. Theo came often and was allowed to have dinner with me one night – turkey and ice cream. They fed me well, and I got stronger every day.

After two weeks I was able to go home, though in a weak condition as regards my organs. The doctor warned me to be very careful as it would take a long time for the uterus to contract and I must not be on my feet. He also warned me not to attempt another baby for a long time. The house seemed very quiet when I got home, with no babies around. The faithful Tilly had returned and the women of the parish had had a new floor laid in the kitchen and had stocked the pantry with provisions. I was so used to the electric lights that it seemed very dark just with oil lamps and of course I missed the nursing and attentions, so I fear I was a little spoiled. I was so lonesome without the children and Tilly begged so for them that Theo set out to bring them home. Grandma came with them to South Norwalk and Theo met them there and brought them across the sound on the steamer. It was very rough and the chairs in the cabin got loose and went tearing around. Nan got her fingers pinched in one of them and Alice was sick over her best dress. They did not enjoy the trip at all and the papa was quite exhausted.

Grandma reported that they had been good, but I know she had her hands full, for Alice was not quite three and Nan four and one-half, and she had to look after their clothes and see that they did not take cold. Alice had a habit of bed-wetting which seemed hard to overcome. Grandma said she would lecture herself when she went to bed, saying, "I will not wet Grandma's bed," and sometimes she got through safely. Mother said Alice looked out over the hill and said, "That's the hospital where mama is – she's gone to get well." They did not undeceive her as it seemed to give her pleasure.

They were so glad to get home, their eyes fairly shone with delight. They hugged and kissed me and said I was a dear, sweet, pretty mama. Tilly was glad to get them again and was quite devoted to them, especially Alice. She would say, "Oh, you sweet child. You never do anything wrong!" She thought

Nan was always getting into mischief, and raised a loud cry one day when the small girl put Alice's wet panties on the hot stove to dry and burned them up. Being reprimanded she said calmly, "It's no matter, she has fourteen pairs."

We settled down to ordinary life again, and it was so nice not to have a great worry on my mind. I still had to be patient and lie down a great deal. In the fall I got well enough to make a visit home, the first since we had moved to Huntington. Sister Kate and Brother Ben had been married during that time and I had been unable to go to the weddings.

Then along in the winter I became aware that I had not followed Dr. Thomas's advice and another baby was on the way. I must say I did not feel very happy about it at first. I would have welcomed a little longer respite but as I improved in health I was glad, and Papa once more looked forward to a boy. I knew I would have to be extremely careful if I were to avoid a repetition of the trouble, so I made up my mind to a very quiet summer. I did not even go out to ride, but just lay in the hammock and took life easy. I grew properly this time, and my baby clothes were all ready, so I had not much to worry about.

Tilly departed as she could not stand sleeping so near the grave yard, for fear of ghosts. We had good Katie in the kitchen and the little girls were old enough to take care of themselves a good deal.

That fall we took in a school teacher to board, a nice girl named Laura Marsh. The children got quite attached to her and called her Aunt Lola.

In October my time was at hand and the doctor said I had nothing to fear. It seems to me now quite remarkable that I trusted Dr. Banks again to see me through. He engaged a nurse for me who proved to be a match for him in being behind the times.

On the eighteenth of October, I waked the father at five

o'clock as usual and told him it was time to get the doctor. While he was gone my pains came on badly and when he got back it was evident that the baby was not going to wait for the doctor. I told Theo I must have a woman right away, and he went to a neighbor at a farmhouse across the street and begged her help. She came and between them they managed to deliver the baby. I'm sure it was very unprofessional and I was terrified when they told me the cord was wound around the baby's neck, but they succeeded in getting it unwound. Mrs. Sweeney took the baby away into the bathroom and she squalled, so I was relieved. Poor Papa exclaimed, "Another girl!" but I was so thankful to have a live baby that I did not care which it was. Dr. Banks arrived out of breath, and I begged him to look at the baby and be sure it was all right. He said, "I'll look at you first," and proceeded to finish up the amateur work. Mrs. Sweeney washed and dressed the baby and went home and I lay alone with her cuddled tight to me until the nurse came. There had been a great commotion in the house that morning. A piece of ceiling fell in my room, almost over the bed. The kitchen sink was stopped up and the plumber was sent for. It was St. Luke's day and the parson had to hold a service. Everybody was rushing around, the children much excited. We said the baby ought to be a doctor or a nurse, as she came on St. Luke the physician's day.

As soon as I looked at the nurse I knew I was in for an uncomfortable time. She was tall and bony, and had a severe countenance, hair strained back and wound in a knot at the back of her head. She looked as if she never smiled and I thought longingly of my cheery Aunt Sarah. We had the big divan put in my room for her to sleep on and she certainly did sleep, not to say snore, and I could hardly wake her. When the baby cried she brought her to me to nurse and then went to sleep again. She was so cross at being waked that I let the baby stay and nursed her again when she waked up instead of having her moved to the other side. The consequence was that my neglected breast got swollen and abscessed. The doctor prescribed a peppermint liniment to rub on it and the Gamp said, "I knew a woman who used that and it drove the milk to her brain and she was crazy as a loon." This did not alarm me and I laughed muchly to myself at the thought of milk on the brain.

I have a memory of that stiff, gaunt figure, standing in front of the bureau in the morning, tightening up her stays – girding on her armor for the day.

My life was most uncomfortable, what with the pain and the fever and worry about the baby who cried every night. The creature sat up with her, grimly rocking, while I suffered with a desire to take the baby myself and soothe her. The nurse remarked in the morning that she could have stopped her but she knew her mother wouldn't allow it. I suppose she referred to Winslow's soothing syrup or paregoric and I'm glad she knew enough to be sure I wouldn't allow that.

Marion Peck came on to keep house and she and Miss Marsh tried to manage the small girls, and encountered some rebellion. There was trouble in the kitchen between the maid and nurse and they all brought their quarrels to me. Marion would come up on the morning with pad and pencil and ask me what to order and what to have for dessert and tell me everything that went on. It made my fever worse, and my head was so tired I felt as if I could not stand it. My breast had to be lanced several times and I had a great deal of pain.

Then all of a sudden the creature (I have even forgotten her name) left me because her next patient came on too soon. She packed her bag and departed leaving the baby unwashed and me half attended to, but I heaved a sigh of relief to see her go. Theo was furious and went and got Mrs. Sweeney for the day, and then telegraphed St. Luke's hospital in New York to send out a nurse at once. So I had my first trained nurse and she was such a comfort. She nearly exploded with wrath when she saw what a condition I was in, said if a hospital nurse had allowed a patient to have a "broken breast" she would have been dismissed in disgrace. She fixed me up beautifully, kept the family out of my room, soothed the baby at night with a bottle of warm water, and I felt a great sense of relief. I had the old weakness again when I tried to get up, so I was kept in bed most of the time for five weeks.

We had to decide on a name for the new baby and could not think of anyone we wanted to name her for, so I said I would select a name I liked and call her Marjorie. It made me think of the sweet marjoram of the old gardens and I knew she was going to be a sweet child, so they let me name her and added Ruth as a middle name, that being a family name on the Peck side. Harriet said I spoiled two pretty names by putting them together. As soon as I was well enough to go to church she was baptized, and Aunt Clara and Aunt Lola were Godmothers, and Hiram Paulding Godfather.

The little girls were much excited about the baby sister. Alice was a great lap girl and even at four years like to sit in my lap while I read stories. When told she had a baby sister, she calmly remarked, "There'll be two in the lap now." She had no idea of giving up her place.

As I had only one good breast and had to begin feeding Marjorie, the first time I had been obliged to use a bottle, and now my troubles began. There were no scientific rules for baby feeding within my reach, so I had to put up with Dr. Banks's directions. We got milk from across the street where there were no modern sanitary conditions, just an ordinary barnyard, nothing sterile, milk brought in a tin pail. It did not agree with the baby, and I tried several prepared foods, but she did not grow and was evidently running down. I got much worried and wished someone would tell me what to do. Then a friend gave me a copy of a magazine called "Babyhood" published by the best child specialists in New York, in which were articles on every subject connected with child nurture, and to which mothers could submit their problems and get answers.

I subscribed to it at once and was so thankful for its guidance. An article on baby feeding recommended sterilized milk – no mention of Pasteurizing at that stage of the game – and told where to get a sterilizer and how to prepare the milk. I sent for one at once and then spent my mornings cooking and bottling and cooling the milk. I found it convenient to have the whole day's supply put up at once. The milk agreed with the baby and she began to improve right away and was a very sweet baby.

In the winter I got worried about Alice, for she had incessant colds, coughed quite badly, slept with her mouth open and snored loudly. Her chest was falling in and she was pale and miserable. The doctor tried tonics without much success. Then once more "Babyhood" came to my rescue. An article by Dr. Delevan (the name has just been dragged up from my subconscious) described a condition called enlarged adenoids which had just been discovered. He described Alice's condition so exactly that I felt sure that was her trouble and I did so wish I knew where to find that doctor. I had no idea how to get at him and Dr. Banks was no help – he had never heard of adenoids.

I felt we must do something as the little girl was running down fast. Theo thought of Dr. Charles Scudder, Ed's brother, who was practicing in New York, and he wrote and asked him what we ought to do. He replied that the child surely should have attention and if we would bring her to his office he would examine her and give his advice.

I got Mrs. Cox, our trained nurse to come and stay with Marjorie and we took Alice and Nan on the morning boat to New York. Nan did not want to miss anything so exciting as a boat trip to New York, and we thought we might have time to go to Central Park, so we let her come along.

We found Dr. Scudder's office and the office boy reported that the doctor had been called to court as a witness and would not be back for some time, but wanted us to wait. After sitting there a long time the children got restless, it was lunch time and we began to fear we would miss the afternoon boat. I had noticed on coming in that there were two doctors' names on the door and that a door opened from the waiting room into the other office. I heard a doctor come in there and asked the office boy his name. "Dr. Delevan, a nose and throat specialist," he said. I said, "That's just what I want, do you think he would see me?" He said: "Well, they are very particular not to take each other's patients but perhaps he would."

I ventured to knock on the door and was admitted and told the doctor how it was, that we had come a long way to see Dr. Scudder and were afraid we might have to leave if he did not come soon.

He said they made it a rule not to see each other's patients, but under the circumstances he would examine the child and report to Dr. Scudder.

I took Alice in and told him about her and that I had been convinced by an article in Babyhood that she had large adenoids. He said, "I wrote that article and it has brought me more patients than anything I ever wrote for the Medical Journal." I told him how much I wanted to see him but had no idea how to find him and he acknowledged that it was a happy coincidence. He said the only cure was an operation and he would talk with Dr. Scudder and let me know what they decided. He told me he was the only doctor doing that operation in New York, that there was one in Brooklyn and one in Boston. The operation had just come into use and no New York hospital would allow him to operate as he was not on their staffs, so it would have to be private.

We had time to go to the park and eat our lunch and then took the boat home. The next day Dr. Scudder wrote that he would engage a room for us at the Park Avenue Hotel near his home, and he and Dr. Delevan would come there and operate. He set the day and said that if we would come down in the morning he would operate in the afternoon.

We went down and found the old hotel (now demolished). Our rooms were on the top floor and the doctors had ordered a table, pails, and basins brought up.

Alice was such a simple, trusting child that she asked few questions, just took things for granted, and amused herself by perching on the broad window seat and looking on things in the street while I held on to her dress. The Papa and I took turns going down to lunch, and she thought it strange that she could not have any, but was comforted by the promise of ice cream "by and by."

The doctors came at two o'clock and she was undressed and given the ether in her bed, so she would not be frightened at the table. I watched her go under ether and then they carried her to the table and I was asked to wait in the other room.

The operation took about twenty minutes and she came out of it crying and thrashing about so that Papa was asked to come in and quiet her. I suppose she felt as much abused as they all do when they have been so imposed on. She was sick all the afternoon but slept well at night and in the morning was allowed ice cream but was much disgusted because it had ground up macaroons in it and she did not like these. The weather was extremely hot and when the doctors came to see her they thought she was too wilted to go home that day, but we felt we must go, so took the afternoon boat home.

Dr. Delevan prescribed nose spray and cod liver oil and iron tonic and said it would take a while for her to pick up.

Already she slept without snoring and that was a great improvement. I was so thankful, for he said she would have been a chronic patient if she had not been relieved. It seems strange now, when tonsils and adenoids are an everyday operation, performed by almost any doctor in his office, that Alice should have been one of the first children to go through it. So once more my little magazine was a life saver.

We were a happy family, all well now, Nannie and Alice growing prettier all the time, and Marjorie the sweetest baby. Her fair hair and skin, and deep blue eyes made her a little beauty. Some admiringly said she was like a little piece of Dresden china. She had a dimpled chin and lovely smile and was as plump as a little cherub.

Nan and Alice did not go to school as there was none near enough, but Nan learned to read and was soon devouring books at her own disposition. I kept up the readings of child classics, which I enjoyed as well as they, and Alice could still sit in my lap if she wanted to.

We had acquired a family carriage, a big heavy thing with doors, so we could all go to ride, and made many trips to the beaches. In the winter our good old black Gypsy had departed. He got some kind of sore on his leg and was out of health, so the Vet said he ought to be put out of the way. It was hard to part with him, and when he marched off gallantly to his execution, his head held high, and the same prancing gait, we felt like shedding a tear.

Bishop Littlejohn, through a friend, secured the gift of another horse for the Parson, as he knew he needed one. She was the wickedest little mare that ever a poor parson had to struggle with. Her name was Jenny, or Lady Jane, and she had plenty of feminine traits; she was tricky, sly, and undependable. It was winter when she arrived, and Theo harnessed her to the sleigh and drove her to the village as a test – she kicked up her heels and ran every step of the way. He was quite dismayed, but got her somewhat tamed so she was safe to drive the family. But if we went down a steep hill and she felt the carriage pressing on her, up would go her heels and I would hold my breath for fear we all would go over the dash-board.

We also acquired a maid, who ought to go on record as having missed her profession. She should have been a writer of dime novels or a movie actress. She managed to fool us into believing there were burglars in the house every night. We would find things in the kitchen and pantry all mixed up, and some articles of food missing. Sometimes these would be discovered in the furnace or other strange place. It looked to us like the work of a crazy man. She told great tales of what she saw and heard and got us so stirred up that Theo had a burglar alarm set in the cellar and pantry but it never went off and no one but Mamie heard the suspicious noises. It was a pity we didn't have a detective like Jennifer Jones in the house. We did not discover until long afterwards that she hid the things herself and did it just for a sensation.

That summer Theo went to Convention and met his friend, Fred Gardiner, rector of Pomfret Church, and they cooked up a scheme whereby each could have a vacation without much expense. Mr. Gardiner's family wanted to go to the seashore and he suggested that he and Peck exchange parishes for a month, each taking the other's rectory and maids. I felt rather dubious about it as I did not know Mrs. Gardiner and I was suspicious as to how Mamie would behave. But we all wanted to do it so it was decided and we went to the hill country and they came to the shore. They brought their nurse with them so they scored one on me who had no nurse. Their two boys were the ages of Alice and Marjorie and young Merrick was quite a handful. He scandalized the church people by yelling and having tantrums outside during church time. Miss Anna and Miss Emma wanted to spank him. His mother was bringing him up on the modern idea of self-expression.

We felt very grand in the Pomfret stone Rectory with two maids. Here I scored one on Mrs. Gardiner. I never learned until afterwards what she went through with Mamie. She was too polite to tell me, but after I got back I found out that Mamie had kept up her underhand ways. I found things all turned about, furniture moved and some things lost. Mamie had the face to tell me the greatest yarns about Mrs. Gardiner moving everything and finding fault with the house, and she confided to me that Mrs. Gardiner was "cracked in the head." I had not yet discovered Mamie's perfidy, so I thought Mrs. Gardiner must be a strange person. Sometime later when we got acquainted I was told the true tale of her troubles in our house. I had been rather worried that the children would spoil things in Mrs. Gardiner's fine house, so much better than ours. In fact they did spill blackberry juice on her fine table linen.

We little knew when we made this exchange visit that it would be a turning point in our lives. While in Pomfret Theodore drove to Brooklyn, a few miles north to see Archdeacon Jarvis. He found Bishop Williams there, hiding at his favorite retreat, the Brooklyn rectory. He and the Archdeacon were discussing a new move in the Diocese, the employment of a general Missionary to Eastern Connecticut who would have no parish and be free to travel all through the region, look up the lonely church people and select hopeful centers for new Mission work. They felt that part of the state was being neglected, and as the towns were far apart and the people scattered, it would take the whole time of one man to look after the work. There were only a few settled parishes in that part of Connecticut – in great contrast to the western part of the state where there is an Episcopal church in most every village. They had been assured the salary if the right man could be found, but no one wanted to do it. Would Theodore Peck undertake it?

His missionary spirit and innate love of adventure rose to

the challenge. He was getting a little tired of his routine work and being subservient to the Vestry and liked the idea of being his own master responsible only to the Bishop, and allowed to work out his own ideas. Then too, he had never paid his debt of gratitude to Bishop Williams who had been like a father to him in his young days, got scholarships for him and was very fond of him. He used to tell me he was dandled on the Bishop's knee when he was a small boy and the Bishop had always been good to him. Then as soon as he was ordained, he was called to the New York diocese and then Long Island, so he had never worked under his own Bishop and he thought Bishop Williams felt hurt about it. So here was his chance to repay this debt before the Bishop died, and to do something that he specially wanted done. They saw that he was attracted by the offer and explained their ideas to him. They told him the salary would be one thousand dollars with two hundred for house rent and two hundred for the horse's keep. We were getting twelve hundred in Huntington and no fund for the horse, so it would be practically the same. Before the conference was over, he had practically promised to take the Job.

The next step was to get my consent and when we got back to Pomfret he broke the news to me cautiously. My first sensation was of my heart descending to the sole of my boots, as it always did when the word "move" was mentioned. Oh, why must I be torn up again when I had enjoyed seven lovely years of peace, though broken into by illness. It was such a lovely place to bring up children. I felt sure more were coming and what would I do with the father away half the time, living in lonely places far away from my friends and not belonging anywhere. The people in Huntington were so good to me, and I loved the church and services and had made some dear friends. Why must I be torn up by the roots again?

Theo reasoned with me gently and said, "You know, Nan, you were willing to go to China if I had passed the physical examination, and this will be near home and in the same state with both our families, and I will have a chance to do a piece of work that needs doing and no one else wants to do." I agreed to that and reminded myself of the resolution I had made when we were married that I would never object to going where the work called: "Whither thou goest, I will go" should be my motto.

Before we went home to Huntington it was practically settled that he would accept the appointment and begin the first of November. I was anxious to know where we were to go at first and what we would live in – no more rectories for us. Mr. Jarvis arranged that we should rent a farmhouse owned by one of the Pomfret parishioners, half a mile from the church and rectory where we had stayed. The owner was willing to let the missionary occupy it for one year. (Oh, yes, I thought, keep on moving!) There was a barn for Jenny, and we could have the milk from one cow and keep chickens. The hired man could milk the cow and keep on sleeping in a back room over the shed. It was rather a blow to my pride to be living in a farmhouse instead of a rectory and not to belong anywhere. Bishop Brewster's wife once told me that one of the hardest things when the Bishop left his parish was not belonging anywhere.

The next step was to break the news to the parish, and it was received with consternation and entire lack of understanding. Miss Emma said, "Why in the world do you want to leave us and go into the wilderness? If you were called to a larger parish we could understand it, but this seems so foolish." Miss Anna, good soul, had more of a missionary spirit and commended the Rector, though she could hardly bear to part with us.

The vestry of course accepted the resignation, with regrets and entire lack of comprehension, and we began to make preparations to move. I was to go with the children to Groton and stay with the Peck family while Theo moved the goods and Jenny across the sound by boat to South Norwalk, then he would drive diagonally across the whole state of Connecticut to Pomfret in the northeast corner.

His mother had died but father and sister were living in a nice new rectory and had room for us. Mamie had consented to go with us. We had not yet discovered her perfidy and lived to rue the day we took her.

The last Sunday came, and it was a very trying day, saying our farewells and listening to dire predictions as to what would happen to us in the wilds of Connecticut. You might have thought we were to meet rattlesnakes or Indians.

The Parson had some nice presents, one from a woman who loved horses and provided for Jenny's comfort by the gift of a large, warm horse blanket, adding also a lap robe for the missionary. The St. Agnes guild made him a set of small linens for house services and gave him a small silver-plated communion set, packed in a box for traveling. I can't remember whether I had any presents but I'm sure the Pauldings would have given me something.

It was hard to say my goodbyes and leave my comfortable, happy home for an unknown life. I felt then and still feel that it was a mistake to appoint a man to that work who had three children and more to follow, a wife who had spent half of her married life being sick, and a man whose eyes were imperfect, with the assurance that they would grow worse. I told Theo the family would be a millstone around his neck – and it often proved a true prophecy. However, the die was cast and I girded on my armor, and determined not to have too many regrets. So it was good bye to Huntington, and our seven peaceful years.

Part II

Missionary Years – Expanding the Church in Rural Connecticut

Pomfret and Putnam 1892-1895

We moved on Monday morning: a great mistake – don't do it. After a Sunday of heart-rending farewells, with people coming and going all afternoon, to get the trunks packed, lay out children's things for the journey and get them up and dressed early in the morning, eat a scrambled breakfast with most of the dishes packed up, then drive three miles to get the early train, was a pretty nerve-wracking work. Marjorie was one year old, and I had to provide food for her, Alice was five and Nan seven, both much excited and racing around.

Mamie was to go with us and we left the Papa to pack the last things and get the household goods to the boat. He drove us to the station and put us on the train and then went back to the house. It was not so simple going to New York in those days. We had to ferry from Long Island City, then look up the baggage and recheck it, and get across the city to the Grand Central by horse car. We took train for New London, arriving at Groton in the evening, tired, dirty and hungry.

Before Theo got back from the station the men had loaded the last things on to the wagon and tied up the remnants, such as dustpans, brushes and pans in an old quilt. They even put in a bottle of iodine which, of course, spilled and spoiled everything. It was a real man's move. Theo helped load the goods on the schooner which was to take them across to Norwalk, and then he took the steamer with Jenny and the two-wheeled gig, which he had purchased for his missionary journeys. He also had to move the family carriage and drove the whole outfit across the state to Pomfret, taking several days. He had some adventures on the way, naturally, which was what he liked. The episode on East Haven Green was not so enjoyable however. They met a steam roller, an abomination which Lady Jane could never abide, and always refused to pass. She balked, and Theo got out and covered her head with the blanket and tried to pull her past it, but she kicked so he had to give it up. She began running backward and he held her head while she backed the whole outfit all around the Green. He held on and managed to prevent either of the vehicles from being upset – pretty clever, I say, and how the little boys must have laughed! He never forgot that experience and related it with great gusto every time we passed East Haven Green in after days.

When the furniture had arrived in Pomfret, he sent me word to come up on the train and he met me and the children at the station. It was a cold November morning and things looked pretty bare and uncomfortable when I arrived at the farmhouse where we were to live. There were piles of boxes everywhere, nothing unpacked, furniture not in place, just heaps, and confusion. The house was not warm and the baby took cold and had an attack of croup. It was too cold for her upstairs and I spent the first few days sitting in the corner by the big coal stove, holding her, wrapped in a blanket. Our first visitor was the village doctor, and I know he sympathized with me as he surveyed the piles of boxes. Then Theo got to work opening them and ran a sliver into his thumb which caused a felon and required the doctor's services. This put the work back and it seemed as if we would never get settled. I felt like a cat in a strange garret, so lonesome and lost.

There was some furniture in the house so that with what we brought we were fairly comfortable, when at last things were in place. The large room with the coal stove was dining, sitting room and nursery. There was a room which we called a study, where the bookcases and desk were kept, but it was too cold to use in winter and the parson had no time for study. The bedrooms were cold but we put a small coal stove in my room and there the whole family had to bathe and dress. There was a line of sheds hitched on to the house which extended almost to the barn.

Jenny had a good stall in the barn and we were allowed the milk of one cow. The hired man milked and took care of the animals, so that was a little help. We had thick yellow cream for breakfast which compensated for the lack of some other things. I could even make butter by shaking the cream in a fruit jar, and when Bishop Williams visited the rectory I had the honor of making a pat of sweet butter for him. It hurt my pride a little to be making butter for the Bishop in a farm house instead of entertaining him in a rectory, but that was one of the new things I had to become accustomed to.

We were not troubled with callers and I had no parishioners to think of so I could devote myself to getting settled, and I began lessons with the little girls as there was no school near enough for them. They had been rather isolated in Huntington also and it was bad for them. They were getting very shy and timid, having no playmates or school and I was glad when the doctor's little girls came and made their acquaintance, Margaret and Leslie Sawtelle, their first real friends. Even so they were painfully shy if they were invited to a party with other children. It was only a short way up the hill to the Sawtelles but they were afraid to go alone because of a rude boy who came out and threatened to hurt them. I went a little way with them and then stood and watched, but I encouraged them to stand up for themselves and not be so afraid.

Mrs. Gardiner was nice to me and invited me to Auxiliary meetings but I felt too out of place to go much. I took the small girls to church but there too I felt lost and as if I did not belong. Theo was away every Sunday getting his work started. I left Marjorie with Mamie and now her evil character began to show. She left off her disguise and showed herself a slattern and was very unruly. I knew she had her friends in as soon as I left the house: provisions disappeared and one day she brought a girl friend to her room and hid her there several days, taking up meals to her before I found it out.

One Sunday I came home and found the kitchen full of Irishmen, all smoking pipes, and my baby in her highchair smothered in tobacco smoke. The remains of a meal were on the table. Nan and Alice were upstairs in bed with colds, and told me there had been a great hurrah in the kitchen all the morning. My wrath rose and I went down and told the men to go at once, and I told Mamie she might go too. She packed up and left and I locked the door on the whole crew and felt I was mistress in my own house.

Theo made some exploring trips that fall, but the days were short and he soon had to stop and wait for spring. The Bishop wanted him to concentrate on two places that winter, Black Hall on the shore where he could go by train, and Putnam, a mill town five miles from Pomfret. He went to Black Hall twice a month and stayed at Black Hall School with Mr. and Mrs. Charles Bartlett. They were earnest church people and held Episcopal services at the school Sunday evenings. There was no church of any kind in Black Hall and they saw great need for mission work among the poor people, many of them as primitive as those in the southern mountains, whole families living in one-room cabins. They had no religious influence and there was much immorality.

The Bartletts were raising money for a mission building and asked the new missionary to take it up and push it, so he made it a major endeavor that winter.

In Putnam a great mistake had been made. The Missionary Society of the Diocese in celebrating some Centennial had put up a large church building in the center of the business district. For a few years they had a good man there and the work prospered, and then through the pig-headedness of a young ritualist, who tried to force high church customs on the people, such as compulsory confession and fasting Communion, the congregation was broken up and the work closed. The Bishop wished it re-opened and the mission put on its feet, so Theo went at it and spent much time there, looking up the scattered people and trying to win them back to their Church.

He took me over one day to see the church. It was quite handsome, though very dark – heavy black walnut fittings and no light from the stained-glass windows. It was a sorry sight, dust and cobwebs everywhere, prayer books lying in the seats, moldy and mildewed. In the vestry room were the remains of the last Communion service, moldy bread and things strewn around as if they had been left suddenly, like the ruins of Pompeii. It was a scene of desolation and the parson's soul rose up in indignation and he determined to put things right. He rounded up the old members and got the women interested in getting the church cleaned, then he began having regular services and by Easter, when I went over with him, he had a good congregation, Sunday School, organist and choir. They had a good service and several baptisms, and the work seemed to be well-launched. The people were glad to get back to their own church and have a minister they could trust.

The first of December I had an urgent invitation from my father to come home for Christmas and bring the family. I had been home very little and now that there was no water to cross and the train went right through from Pomfret to Waterbury, he thought I might manage it and he would pay the car fare. I jumped at the chance, for I had not been home for Christmas since I was married, and all my brothers and sisters were in Waterbury at that time, Ben and Lil living upstairs in Father's house, Fred and Helen next door, Kate and Frank a few houses on the other side, Mary in her new school nearby. One of my mother's friends said she was like a hen with her chickens all around her, she only had to say "cluck, cluck," and they would run home – all but me.

My parents felt that changes were coming and this might be the last time the family could get together and so it proved, for by another Christmas some had moved away and the separation had begun. The only drawback was that Theo could not go with us, as he had service in Putnam in the morning, but he could take the afternoon train and be there for the tree in the evening.

The little girls were much excited at going to Grandma's and set to work making Christmas cards and little presents for Grandma and Aunties. I racked my brains as to what I could do for presents, as I had little money and no place to shop. I contrived some small fancy work and made rag dolls and stuffed animals for the various babies, Dorothy, Harold, Margaret, Teddy and Marjorie. I made an elephant and a pig, a rabbit and a Chinaman with pigtails, and for Marjorie a wonderful cat made from an old fur lining. It had green glass beads for eyes and was quite a work of art. She loved it and always took it to bed.

I went to Putnam and got some dolls to dress for Nan and Alice, as it was an established custom that Christmas meant new dollies. They both loved dolls and played with them a great deal.

I was wonderfully thrilled at the thought of going home

and realized how lonely I had been. Theo took us to the train two days before Christmas in a buggy which he had bought to replace the big family carriage, as Jenny always kicked going down hill when the heavy carriage pressed on her, and that was decidedly unpleasant for the passengers. It was crowded in the buggy, baby in lap, Alice between us and Nan on the floor with the baggage.

We were warmly welcomed in Waterbury, but it was miserable rainy weather, a real grippe season, and when Nan and Alice went shopping with Aunt Kate, Nan fell down in the mud and spilled a bag of peppermints, to her great grief. They had supper with Aunt Kate and told me with great enthusiasm about a great cake "all highed up with chocolate" which Auntie made. They seldom saw a layer cake in our house.

We had a big family Christmas dinner and kept some for Theodore until he arrived in the afternoon. In the evening there was a big tree upstairs in Aunt Lil's room, which she and Kate decorated. Grandpa dressed up for Santa Claus and there was a merry time. Poor Grandma, after cooking for all those people and managing everything, was taken sick in the evening with chills and fever, and the doctor pronounced it a bad case of grippe. We went home as soon as possible to get out of the way, leaving Mary to nurse Grandma.

This visit made a bright spot in the long winter, as Christmas always does, and helped me to endure the cold and loneliness better.

When spring came Theo started out on his exploring trips again, between Sundays which were still devoted to Putnam and Black Hall. He always tried to get home before dark but was always getting caught and either had to feel his way home or find a place to stop for the night. I still felt very strongly that it was a mistake to appoint a man for that work who had poor eyesight, and so much family, but on the other hand a single man would have found it hard not to have a home to come to for rest and comfort between times. Sometimes the night was passed in a small country hotel, with cold rooms, hard beds and greasy fried foods. Sometimes a friendly farmhouse took him in, but he had to answer a great many questions before they would trust him. He wore the clerical vest and collar, as a badge of good character, but even so they were suspicious. He had a card printed, "Theodore M. Peck, General Missionary", but the printer made a mistake and put it "Gospel Missionary", so they took him for a Salvation Army man. He had to explain himself constantly and met with entire ignorance as to what an Episcopal minister meant. If he spoke of the Bishop having sent him, they did not know what the word meant. When he entered a village he went to the Post Office and asked if there were any Episcopalians in the town. They practically said "There ain't no such animal." It took a good while to locate our scattered people but when he did find them they were delighted to see him and to let him hold a service for them and any who would come. He baptized the babies and celebrated the Holy Communion for those who had so long been deprived of it. The silver and linens given him by the Guild in Huntington were very useful in this way. He left literature and prayer books wherever he went and promised to visit the families as often as he could. He saw many villages where no religious services were held, and sometimes there would be an abandoned church building or old "meeting house" where he could gather a congregation and have a service. He used the Evening Prayer leaflets which had the psalms and hymns printed in proper order, so they did not need to be confused by trying to find places in the prayer book. Sometimes he gathered a congregation in the parlor of a hotel, next the bar-room, and sometimes in a school house or town hall. As a rule he found the country people glad of a chance to go to a religious service, though the Episcopal Church was new to most of them.

In driving through the country on Sunday he saw men at work in the fields just as on other days and learned a good deal about the ignorance and low morality of the countryside. They needed help both in religious and social life. He also found some spots which were hopeful for opening new work – church people who were rejoiced that their Church was remembering them. One of these was in Hampton and one in Jewett City, among the English factory hands.

He tried hard to find a stopping place before night, but often failed to do so and when he asked admittance to some friendly looking place, he was often refused, as the owners were suspicious of him in spite of his credentials. I suppose they thought no reliable minister would be travelling around that way at night. Often the dogs chased him away before he could get to the door of a house. He always said he had a sympathy for tramps, knowing how it felt to have darkness fall and no place to stay. In our after life he would never turn a tramp away who was looking for lodging. He would take him into our house, or go out and find a place for him. Many a night I have lain awake, wondering whether the sleeping visitor was genuine or whether he might get up and attack us in the night. Once in Piermont three men came just at night who said they were brick layers, travelling from Haverstraw to New York, looking for work and wanted a place to sleep. We had an unused bedroom and Theo put an old mattress on the floor and let them sleep there. In the morning we offered them breakfast, and they insisted on washing up before they accepted. I wanted Theo to turn the key in their door but he would not, so I lay awake, not having quite so much faith in human nature as he had.

The gig was very useful on these long trips. It was easy to pull and would not sink in mud. There was room in the back for his books and papers and his lunch. He liked to tell the children how his bottle of milk was churned into butter by the rough roads he went over. That showed what rich milk we had.

If Jenny had been a proper horse she would have brought him home when he got caught in the dark, but being such a naughty jade she led him on wild goose chases instead of bringing him home. As soon as twilight fell and she felt the reins slacken, she knew he could not see and she got him lost many times. She would turn in to every barnyard, looking for oats, and stop when she thought she had found a good place to stay. He was always getting out to turn her around and inquire the way from someone, till he was tired and dizzy.

One night he was very late and I was out by the road looking anxiously for him, as I had to do so often. At last I saw him coming, walking and dragging the horse by the bridle. He said she had taken him into a number of barn yards and finally into a mill pond to get a drink. He had to back her out, getting wet up to his knees. He was so mad and disgusted with her that having been put on the right road he would not try to drive any longer, but walked and pulled her by the bridle. He surely was a mad parson that night and I know he felt like giving her a good thrashing, but he restrained himself and gave her oats. He was almost too tired and wrought up to eat the supper I had kept hot for him. Jane was no kind of a mare for a poor missionary.

The work at Black Hall was increasing and they were putting up a building to be called the Guild Room. It had a chancel at one end which could be shut off by a curtain between Sundays and the room used for social doings. I learned afterwards that this style of building was being much used by our western missionaries. There was a small library in the room, and later on a sewing school was started and evening entertainments held for the neighborhood. Theo also held services in the schoolhouse at South Lyme and in a hotel at Niantic. All this kept him very busy and he was hardly ever at home, so I had all the care of the family.

Our farmhouse was quite pleasant in summer and the row
of great maples in front gave good shade. We had a full house,
for my sister Kate wanted to bring her babies to the country for
the hot weather and offered to pay board if we would take her
and them. Little Dorothy was two, a month or so older than
Marjorie, and baby Harold was nine months, very sickly and
pining. Marjorie had learned to walk, though she was a long
time about it. All winter her sisters had tried to teach her,
standing her in a corner and holding out their hands for her to
come. She would stand there stolidly, a fat little cherub, but at
last would take a few running steps with a broad smile and
grasp their hands. Her ankles were small and she was so fat I
would not hurry her, but by summer she was trotting around
outdoors. We had two baby carriages on the long porch and
two toddlers who sometimes had to be tied to a tree to keep
them from running away, when Nan and Alice got tired of
chasing them. The girlies had their friends, "Marg and Les,"
down there a good deal and Merrick Gardiner was sent there
when they wanted him out of the way, so the place was
swarming with children. Passersby wondered if it was an
orphan asylum or a fresh air home.

In August baby Harold was quite sick. He was such a
pathetic little creature, so lifeless that he would not even lift
his hand to brush the flies off his face. I was horrified to find
him fly-specked. We had to keep him in a carriage with
mosquito net over him. Then Marjorie and Dorothy toddled
into the currant bushes and made themselves sick eating green
currants, and one morning Kate was taken with pains and the
doctor said she would lose the expected baby. When he learned
that Harold was only nine months old he said he was glad of it
and had no sympathy for her, but of course she and I felt
differently about it. I had my hands full waiting on her,
washing and dressing three babies and cooking special food for
Harold. We had a maid now, a neighbor called Mary Maher, an

odd character but pretty good help. She did all the cooking but I had to be in the kitchen a good deal, cooking baby foods.

I sent word home about our troubles and word came right back that sister Mary would come to the rescue. I breathed a sigh of relief, for Mary was our great standby, and always a host in herself. She found me with Harold undressed on my lap, trying to bathe him and look after Dorothy at the same time. Mary took right hold and soon had things organized. Someone had to spend hours sterilizing milk for Marjorie, cooking granum for Harold and bottling it all. We had no screens and the flies were terrible, getting into the milk before we could shut it up. I don't know what I would have done without Mary that summer, for in addition to everything else, I had found that another baby was on the way. I had a good deal of sewing to do for myself and the newcomer, and I knew that we must soon be packing up to move again, as our year at this farmhouse was nearly up. At last Kate and Harold got well enough to go home and Mary went with them to keep on nursing.

Now arose the problem as to where we were to live. The Bishop wanted Theodore to move to Putnam and make that his headquarters, devote a good deal of time to that mission and go by train from there to his shore missions. Of course there was no rectory and the trouble was to find a house we could live in. Theo began hunting every time he went over there and sometimes took me with him. It seemed impossible to find anything within our means, and we came home discouraged every day. I began to wonder if I would have any place when my time came. I said to Theo, "Will I have to lie down by the roadside and have my baby?" He laughed at me and told me not to worry, he would surely find a place for me. There was no hospital within reach and at that time we had not acquired the idea that it was best to go to a hospital.

At last our search was successful and we found a small

house just made over from a barn. It stood in a lane back of the street, so that the house was behind those which opened on the street. I said we would be living in the back yard and felt rather humiliated that we should be behind the nice houses instead of living in a rectory on the street. Now that we had a church it seemed as if the minister might have a better situation, but I was thankful to have any place where I could lie down. The house was at least new and clean, though so small that I knew we would be packed in like sardines. I felt like calling it the sardine box but I refrained. There was running water and a bathroom so that was a decided advance over the farmhouse.

We moved the first of October and my time was due the middle of the month so I had only two weeks to get settled. It was rainy when we moved in and the plaster was not quite dry, so Nan caught a big cold and had to be put to bed. As in Pomfret, our first visitor was the doctor. I also had an attack of cramps and was afraid something might happen so I was glad to make the doctor's acquaintance. Theo had already engaged him to take charge of my case. He was Dr. Morrell, a solemn, black-bearded man, but kind and very skillful. He never sent a bill in the seven years he was our doctor, and I pause here to make a note of the kindness and generosity of our doctors, and also the surgeons who treated me. They sent no bills, though we always asked for them and expressed our desire to pay them. One eminent doctor said to Theodore, "Dog don't eat dog." We took it as a professional courtesy, though Theo thought it was a one-sided one as the doctors always did so much for him and he could do nothing for them except to marry or bury them, unless they would come to church and be preached to. Dr. Morrell's wife was a member of our mission and a good worker, but the doctor seldom came to church. It was the greatest help not to have doctor's bills, for it was all we could do to keep up with the other bills.

The doctor warned me to be very careful not to strain

myself getting settled and especially not to reach up, hanging curtains, etc. It really was a pleasure to have a modern, skillful doctor after my experience with Dr. Banks.

I did so want to have a pretty house and I had very little to use for it. There were three rooms downstairs opening together with arches and no doors; a parlor, sitting room and dining room. Also there was a good sized kitchen and pantry. Upstairs were three bedrooms and a tiny room for the maid. One bedroom would have to be used for a study, as there was no room downstairs for desk and books. Marjorie's crib would have to be in my room as also the baby's cradle when he arrived. Nan and Alice slept together in a wide bed in the other room which was very small.

The floors were pine so Theo oiled them and stained them and we did not have to nail down carpets. We managed to squeeze out money enough to put an ingrain art square for the parlor, in blue and gray. I got some short blue silkolene curtains for the windows. Mrs. Gardiner gave me two portiere curtains of gray rep with broad bands of blue satin for a border and I hung one of them between the two front rooms and cut up the other to make cushions for our two good chairs.

I had a small mahogany table and our nice bookcase full of books. The parlor organ had been sent on from my old home and with our good pictures and small ornaments it looked quite tasteful and homelike. It was the nicest-looking room I had had for a long time.

In the sitting room was an old rug, big coal stove, the large divan which Theo built, covered with the Indian blanket given him in Huntington, and which served as a playground for all you children, also two school desks contributed by Aunt Mary when she broke up her school. Nan and Alice kept all their possessions in these. A small bookshelf, round table and a few chairs filled this room full. There was a square window between the dining room and pantry where we could put dishes through, and our maid, Mary Maher, who would have liked to eat with us but was not invited to, would seat herself in the pantry to eat her meals where she could look at us through the window and hear all we said. It annoyed me very much to have her sitting there, like an "owl in an ivy bush." but I put up with it, she was so touchy. She also monopolized the bathroom, being as glad to get a bath as we were, I suppose, and would stay in there by the hour, splashing and muttering to herself. She evidently had an obsession for the bath. I had an idea that she was touched in the head and was not sorry when she decided to go home after a few months.

There was no furnace, and we had the pot-bellied stove in the sitting room and a coal stove in the kitchen as the only heat, and we put a small stove upstairs in my bedroom.

The house was in pretty good order when the time arrived for the new baby. It was a pleasure to me to have it so new and clean, after the messy farmhouse I had lived in. I had a good nurse engaged, a woman about my own age, Miss Heath, who was ready to come when sent for.

At the usual hour of five in the morning I sent Theo for Dr. Morrell, who stayed with me while Theo went for the nurse. She got there just in time. Theo was making a fire in the stove when the doctor said "Here's your boy" and the Papa turned around with a broad grin and felt like shouting "Hoop-la!" At last the boy so long awaited, and his name was ready for him, Theodore Abbott Peck.

Marjorie was asleep in her crib alongside of my bed and did not wake till seven o'clock, when she opened her eyes and smiled shyly when Dr. Morrell spoke to her. He thought she was wonderfully sweet. Theo picked her up and carried her off to her sisters' room and I said, half sadly, "Goodbye baby," and she waved her fat hand goodbye. He put her in bed with her sisters and told them they had a baby brother and they would have to stay home from school that day to take care of Marnie.

They had commenced going to a small private school in the doctor's house and when he came in later they told him proudly that they had to stay home to take care of their little sister. Alice said she didn't mind it except changing Marnie's panties when they did not get her to the chair in time.

I had a comfortable month, with Miss Heath looking after the housekeeping and children, combing the girlies' long hair and seeing that they were dressed for school. Dr. Morrell had asked to have them come to the school at half price, as he knew we could not pay much. He said it was a privilege to have such nice children and I was glad to have them get away from their isolated home life. It was time, for they were six and eight years old and had never been to school, although they could read and had been taught at home. They were still painfully shy about being with other children and I had to go with them the first day and stay part of the morning. It was hard for them to join in the games and songs but when they got used to it they enjoyed going and would repeat the games in the afternoon with Marnie.

After Mary Maher left I had a girl named Maria, a halfwit with a cleft palate who could not speak plainly. She was a good worker but I could not trust her with the baby. Sometimes I had to go downtown on errands and would leave the children together with Nan in charge. The baby lay in his carriage in the living room, one more article of furniture, and I told Nan not to take him up but to push the carriage if he cried and shake his rattle. One day when I came home she told me proudly that she had "changed him" because he needed it. I found she had done it all right and I could trust her better than Maria.

It was a "little house well filled" that winter, and the sitting room got pretty crowded with baby's goods, playthings and sewing but they were all happy. If callers came the little girls would climb up on the couch to be out of the way. The "pretty parlor" was too cold and we had to keep the portieres drawn.

The Congregational minister and his wife called one day, and as they looked around I had an idea they pitied me, but I did not want their pity, even if we were in the back yard while the "Congos" had a nice parsonage on the street.

Our mission was rather looked down upon because the people who came to it were mostly working people. We heard that it was spoken of as the "washerwomen's church," but we felt that that was something to be proud of.

Nan and Alice were going through the paper doll craze and had fleets of them all over the rooms, perched on my plants, on the lamps and everything which furnished a roosting place. They kept them in their desks and were very mad at their little sister when she opened the desks and calmly tore the heads off the paper dolls!

One day the Gilmore's Band came to town and we took the girls to hear the concert. It was their first chance to hear big music, and they were specially thrilled because there was a "princess", a real one, they were sure, who sang the solos. They were perfectly carried away with the music and when they got home went to work to reproduce the entertainment with their paper dolls, making a stunning princess and acting out the concert, playing on combs with paper over them. Imagine the difference from the children of these days, surfeited with music and acting in the movies and on the radio.

Marjorie was a cute little monkey, so round and chubby with lovely blue eyes sparkling with mirth, and fat rosy cheeks. She was full of fun and after dinner every day she would get Nan and Alice to dance with her in the hall, and jump around on her sturdy legs, shouting "Danny, danny, danny." She was the funniest little talker, and got everything twisted. A pin cushion was a "quinpishie" and pumpkin pie was "puckie peow".

I had to sew a great deal making things over, piecing and patching to keep them clothed. I remember how proud I was when I contrived a coat and hood out of a bundle of pieces sent me, which looked so sweet on Marnie that I was as proud as if I had painted a picture. It was made of grey cloth with lining of striped satin from an old petticoat and trimmed with blue plush down the front, edged with grey astrakhan fur, all out of the bundle given me. The hood was of plush trimmed with the fur and was so becoming to her rosy cheeks, with the flaxen hair just showing, that I felt I had really created something. She was a picture at that age and we had her photograph taken. The photographer liked it so much that he put it up in his window, an enlarged copy of it, as an advertisement. A long time afterwards a friend bought it and gave it to us.

When snow came the children had fun sliding down the hill in back of our house where there was a steep slope ending in a field, quite safe. Sometimes Daddy stayed over a few days and would slide with them, lying flat on a big sled inherited from the Peck family, letting them sit on his back, then drag them up the hill. He made a sleigh for Marnie by nailing a soap box on to a sled and I would drag her around, sometimes accompanied by the other two girls. The housewifely neighbors thought it strange that a mother should be out playing with her children in the morning hours.

At Thanksgiving time we had a nice visit from the Peck family, father and three aunties. They found they could come up from New London and go back the same day by train, so they came up and brought the dinner all cooked, a turkey, even the gravy made, ready to warm up and vegetables and pies. We had a merry time. Then at Christmas week they came again on the way to Southboro to see Will's new baby, little Margaret, and stopped over with us to baptize baby Theodore. He was christened on St. Stephen's day in a very cold church, wrapped in blankets. Mr. Gardiner was his Godfather and Aunt Julia his Godmother.

In the spring the mission had grown so well that the

Archdeacon wanted to have a permanent home for the missionary, looking forward to the time when they could have a minister of their own. Theo started out to raise the money for a rectory and was successful in getting enough to start building in the spring. It was a joy to me to think that I was to live in a rectory again, and for the first time my married life I had something to say about the plans and later on was allowed to choose the wall papers, a happiness I had never expected to attain to. The house was to be built on the street a little way beyond us, so I could watch its progress that summer.

The next Christmas was a remarkably happy one. Up to this time we had not entertained any of our friends as for the first time in our history we had no guest room. However, when George and Carrie asked that they might come and spend Christmas with us, and would help with the expenses and did not care where they slept, on a couch or on the floor, we thought it would be fun to have them come. They would of course bring Jean, ten years old, and that thrilled the girls for they would have to sleep three in a bed, which is always a great lark. George and Carrie could sleep on the couch by the stove and keep warm without so many blankets. So we agreed to the plan and went to work to prepare for our guests. I had let Maria go and was doing the work myself but I knew Carrie would help. Nan and Alice polished the silver and I made some cakes and planned what I could do for presents. I had little money and hardly knew what I wanted to choose of the many things the family needed. Then along came one of those nice things which sometimes happened to us and which made me realize how many kind people there are in the world. A rich lady in Pomfret who had known us there and who was interested in the missionary, came to see me and presented me with ten dollars to spend for Christmas. She also brought her little bank full of pennies which she thought the little girls might like to go shopping with. It seems she made a practice of putting all the pennies that passed through her hands in a bank and when it was full gave it to someone. She poured the pennies out on the table for the girlies to count and they were thrilled to find there were three dollars. For the first time they could go shopping for Christmas, as there were good stores in Putnam. I was very happy too and went downtown to spend my money for many things needed as well as presents for the children. Besides new dollies I got some furniture for the dolls and a baby carriage for Marnie which was the joy of her heart. She called it the "doll-go". I also got rubber boots for the girls as our lane was deep in mud or full of puddles or snow most of the time.

Dad was home and the Peck brothers were very hilarious and entered into the children's sports. We had the stockings in the morning and then I had the joy of going to church with Theo as Carrie insisted on staying home and getting the dinner. I remember how very happy I felt that day and with what real joy and enthusiasm I sang the hymns and the Te Deum, and afterwards went around greeting the people. I suppose I must have looked happy for on turning round I met the sarcastic gaze of the treasurer's wife as if she thought I had no right to be so happy. But I was not going to let her spoil my happy day. In the afternoon the brothers put up a nice tree and set it on a stand in such a way that it could revolve. They were very jolly and called it the "Peck brothers' patent tree". It looked very bewitching when decorated with tinsel, lights and presents, and the small ones gazed in wonder when it revolved slowly before their eyes. We had a very gay time and the guests stayed one more night, so the cousins got quite well acquainted.

I got tired of Maria and thought I could do the work myself with the girlies' help. Even at that early age they were willing to help with dishes and baby care, so we got along after a fashion, but with all the cooking and being on my feet so much my

internal organs got out of shape and I had to go to Dr. Morrell
for treatment every three days. I felt very tired and dragged out
and could not walk outdoors so I did not get the fresh air I
needed. Mrs. Gardiner came over to see me and lectured me
about staying in so much, but when I outlined to her my day,
she concluded I had better lie on the bed with the windows
open. It was hard for her with her two maids and nurse to
visualize what I had to do. I finally got another maid from
Pomfret, named Stacia, and she was good help but soon our
troubles began.

So far we had had no real illness, none of the expected
children's diseases, but now scarlet fever appeared in the
house across the street, or rather the lane. One evening Dr.
Morrell came to our door and said that the little girl over there
with whom our children played was down with scarlet fever
and I must keep our children very carefully away from there. It
was past the age when camphor bags were hung around necks
to prevent contagion, and all we could do was to issue strict
orders that no one should go near that house.

All went well until the child was well enough to come
outdoors and then it was hard for the children to keep away
from her. They would stand across the street, and talk to her
and see how near they could get without touching her. The
only time I remember spanking Marjorie was when her sisters
told me she had been in the Burgess house, but it was not she
who was the first victim. Nan came in one evening feeling sick,
after playing down in the swamp and getting wet. She went to
bed aching all over and I thought it might be rheumatic fever
as she had a high fever in the night. Alice slept with her as
there was no other place and I did not feel especially worried
until morning, when she seemed so sick that I knew I must get
the doctor. Theo was away and there was no telephone, so I
walked to his house and told him about it. He came right over
and when he examined her he found a rash just coming out on

her chest and knew what it was. He looked at me and at the other children who were hanging around and said, "Well, we're in for it. Now what can you do with these other children? Can you send them away somewhere?"

I said no, all my relatives had children and would not want to be exposed. Then he said we would have to do our best to protect them, but he realized it would be almost impossible in that small house, rooms so near together, only one bathroom and only me to manage everything. He suggested a nurse, but I was not willing to give Nan up in her first real illness, so I said I would try to get Miss Heath to do the housekeeping and take care of the others and I would shut myself up with Nan.

Stacia immediately went home so we had no help in the kitchen. When Theo came home he was told that he would have to be quarantined so far as going into people's houses was concerned and of course the Black Hall people did not want him down there. The doctor said he might have services in Putnam if he would stay in the chancel and not shake hands with anyone. That left him free to stay at home and help and he and Miss Heath shouldered the burden at once. He helped her do the washing, as of course no one would take it or come to the house. He hung out the clothes and she ironed them, the milk and groceries were left on the porch, and no one came in. The girls had to stay out of school and help look after Marnie and Teddy. He had learned to walk early and was a good little chap with a lovely curly head and a most winsome smile. He had a trick of coming and laying his head on your knee and smiling up at you which his daddy thought most bewitching.

Miss Heath slept in my bed and kept Marjorie and Teddy with her, Alice had the maid's room and Dad slept downstairs on the couch. I suppose I must have put up a cot in Nan's room but I don't remember. I was up at night anyway as Nan was very sick and delirious, crying about the dreadful pictures on the wall and saying her curls were stuck to them and hurt her.

My mind was racked with anxiety for her and the others and I had hard work to control my imagination and not conjecture up dreadful happenings. I hung up sheets wet in Platt's chlorides in the doorway and bathroom and disinfected everything that went in there. I sometimes had visions of them all dead and wrapped in Platt's chlorides, and suffered agonies while I kept my vigil.

We got past the crisis and then I ventured to change all my clothes at night, wrap my head in a disinfected towel and go down and wash the dishes for a change. I did not go near the children and hoped they might escape but when Nan was pronounced convalescent, one morning I heard the baby choking and vomiting and knew he had it.

I rushed in and snatched him from his bed and hugged him, I was so glad to get hold of him again. He was moved into the study and I stayed in there with him. He did not have a high fever but his ears were very bad and I had to sit up all night with him, he cried so. I spent weary days sitting in that little back room, looking out over the meadows and wondered if I would ever get out again.

While he was still pretty sick Alice came down with it and the doctor said we must have a nurse. We got one from a hospital and Alice felt much abused because she could not have Mama as Nan did. I could go in and see her and we gave up all attempts at quarantine in the house as it was no use. Alice was the sickest of the three, the doctor said, and her throat was very bad.

At the height of our troubles came another terrifying thing. Dr. Russell, the health officer, came to our house one night and asked to see Mr. Peck. It seems an old colored woman had died of smallpox in a tenement which had become infected, and had said that she was a member of the Episcopal Church and wanted to be buried with the prayer-book service. Would Mr. Peck undertake to go to the cemetery at night with him and the grave diggers and read the burial service? Of course he said he would and I was once more plunged into terrible anxiety as to what might happen. It seemed enough to have scarlet fever without adding on smallpox.

It was a weird procession that went out to the cemetery at ten o'clock at night: a horse-drawn wagon conveying the pine coffin, driven by a colored man, two Frenchmen with spades over their shoulders, the doctor leading the minister and carrying an oil lantern. The grave was dug and Theo read the service by the light of the lantern which the doctor held. Then Dr. Russell had the grave diggers take off their coats and put them in the grave and fill it up. They were angry about it and the next day came back and dug them up and started another line of smallpox cases!

Theo came home and hung all his clothes out on the back fence, where they stayed for many a day. He took a disinfectant bath and slept downstairs. No harm came of this philanthropy, but it was some days before I breathed easily.

At last the three were convalescent and Marnie had not shown any signs of the disease. I began getting them outdoors, as it was late in May, and then down came Marjorie and she was the reddest little lobster I ever saw. She had high fever and delirium, but no complications and got well quickly.

Now came the question of how to fumigate and clean the house, with the closets full of trunks and clothes and everything so crowded. The clothes lines were filled every day with things put out to air, and we burned the children's toys and some of their books, but it seemed hopeless to really get it clean with us all in it. Theo felt like setting a match to it but that was hardly practical.

Archdeacon Jarvis came to the rescue with the offer of a cottage at Black Point, owned by one of Theo's church people at Niantic. She would let the missionary's family have it for two months, free of rent. This was hailed with joy by all concerned. I was very much worn out and the doctor had insisted on my going somewhere. My treatments had to be given up all through the siege, and I was much run down. The children looked pale and we all needed to get away, so were very thankful to accept the kind offer. Theo would stay behind and see to the fumigating and could come down to the Point when he visited his shore missions.

We packed up the family and Papa escorted us down to Niantic, where we were transported by carriage to Black Point. Before leaving Theo lighted a pound sulphur candle in each room and asked Mr. Burgess, our next door neighbor, to watch that the house did not burst into flames. When he came back he got a man and woman to help him take out all the carpets and bedding and had the house all scrubbed.

How glad I was to get out. I had been nowhere and seen no one all that time and had only taken the air for a few minutes on the porch. The whole episode had been hard on the parson's work. He had not visited his missions or attended to anything but home duties. This was one of the times I had foreseen when the family would be a millstone around his neck. We were both tired but filled with thankfulness that the little ones were all spared and that kind friends had provided us with a vacation. Poor Papa had the worst of it with all that cleaning and taking care of himself in the house. He had to begin his travels and then come home to an empty house and cook for himself.

The new rectory was being built and more money had to be raised to finish it. His work had grown and spread so that he had more places to visit. Jewett City, near Norwich, had a large English population and operatives in the mills and had asked for services. At Noank the ship builders needed missionary work. A chapel was proposed for South Lyme, and in Niantic

Professor McCook of Hartford had held services in his own house and the people were now ready to build a chapel, so the work was calling in all directions!

It was very hot and he overworked in the sun and when he was in Pomfret one day, he collapsed with heat prostration. Fortunately Mr. Gardiner was with him and took him to the rectory and put him to bed. He was pretty sick a few days, the heart affected, and they did not tell me till he was better. I felt as if I were very selfish to be down by the sea and he sick in hot Pomfret. I wanted to go right up but did not dare leave the children. After a week or so he came down to visit his shore missions and stayed a little while with us.

I found there was plenty of work even at the shore. Stacia had been persuaded to come with us but did not like it and threatened every day to go home. She had to sleep in a small place boarded up on the porch and was scared in the night when she heard the waves roar. There was no water in the cottage, just a pump back of the row of houses, which served them all. It had to be carried to the house and heated on the wood stove and it was some big job to do the family wash, no clothes line, just spreading the clothes on the grass, to be tramped over by restless little feet.

The row of cottages was on a high bank just above the rocky shore and the waves washed at the foot of it so we had plenty of music. The beach was so rocky it was not pleasant bathing there, toes were stubbed and feet cut and knees bumped. When Papa came he moved some of the boulders and with the children's help made a nice pool with sandy bottom where the small ones could disport themselves. The real bathing beach was on the other side of the point and we sometimes walked over there, trailing through the hot meadows and huckleberry bushes, being eaten up with mosquitoes, baby riding in the express cart which had to take the place of his carriage. I sometimes ventured to go huckleberrying, but the mosquitoes were so bad I could not rouse any enthusiasm on the part of the girlies, and I did not want Teddy and Marnie devoured, so we dispensed with huckleberries for the most part.

It was fine on our porch in the evening and when the chicks were safely in bed I lay in the hammock and enjoyed the music of the waves and the moonlight on the water. I wished my man could be there, as I always felt lonely without him.

It kept me busy to provide food enough for they had wonderful appetites and supplies were far from us. A grocer came out from Niantic and took orders and if we forgot anything we had to wait till he came again. Mail was brought by grocer or ice man or whoever was coming so it was rather irregular.

It was a beautiful place, three miles straight out from the harbor, water on both sides. I used to love to walk out to the end of the Point and look both ways, the water was so lovely. There was great surf there sometimes. There was an Inn on the end of the Point and some people who stayed there said the beds were so hard they called them East and West Rocks. Our beds were none too comfortable and we were crowded, the two youngest sleeping in my room and the girls in another small one, only two rooms upstairs. Of course they had to have company also and Jean Peck came out from New Haven and was there over Nan's birthday. I managed a little party for them, contrived some kind of a cake, under difficulties, and a few candies, not much in the way of presents. Nan was much surprised and delighted to get a box of candy from Papa, who usually had to be reminded carefully of birthdays.

They all began to look better except Marnie. The fever had left her rather ailing. She lost her lovely red cheeks and was fretful and cross. I imagine she felt that Teddy had taken her place and she couldn't be babied anymore and she didn't feel well so she was unhappy and cried a good deal. Her sisters teased her sometimes and she was the between one, so, poor little soul, she gave way to her feelings and cried.

Young Teddy was quite a care for he was cutting teeth and his digestion was easily upset. It was hard to get the right food for him and his bowels were often out of order, which made more work. He had a sun bonnet which was the joy of his heart and he insisted on never taking it off, day or night. He would yell "Ba-on, ba-on" until we got it for him. The day I washed it he cried until it was dried and ironed. He was cute, though, and even at that early age was a ladies' pet. The Stoddards of New London were in the next cottage and he would climb up their steps every day with "ba-on" and with his ingratiating smile and demand a cracker, which he always got. Mrs. Stoddard thought he was a perfect dear and always wanted him to come.

Rainy days were a problem, all shut up in one room. I did not quite dare to turn them out in the rain, so tried to keep them busy with scrap books, paints, and so forth. But it was close quarters and Baby was always sticking his fingers into the paste or trying to drink the paint water and he and Marnie tumbled around the floor under foot and there was scrapping and howling. At such times I felt like the German woman with a houseful of children who exclaimed, "Leetle childrun, leetle childrun, Mine Gott I get so tired of leetle childrun!" It was a joy when the sun came out and I could turn them all outdoors.

Sundays were trying: I missed church and hadn't much chance to teach the children. We and other families sometimes sat on the edge of the bluff at evening and sang hymns. I often felt that it was something like "shoemaker's children," their father teaching everyone but them. I felt the responsibility and did my best at it but it was none too good.

While there I had to make a sad journey, for my little sister Kate died of tuberculosis. She had been sick since little Dorothy died in the winter and went down very fast. I felt I

must go to the funeral so left the children with Stacia,
promising to come back at night. I had to get up and start at
six o'clock, having a man come out from Niantic to drive me to
the train, which cost three dollars. I was glad to be with the
family in this first break and to see Kate once more, looking so
lovely in her wedding dress with white sweet peas around her.
They were her wedding flowers. They begged me to stay but I
did not dare leave the baby, so went back at evening and
arrived at nine o'clock. They had all gone to bed, having given
up on me, but Stacia got up and made me a cup of tea. I had
not had any supper, so ate some bread and butter and went to
bed tired out. Stacia said they had been good, but the baby ate
paint, which was perhaps the reason he had a restless night
and kept me awake.

I improved in health but was somewhat worried because I
felt symptoms of another pregnancy. I hoped it was not so, as I
felt very unequal to going through it again so soon, but when I
got home and visited the doctor he confirmed my suspicions
and I had to accept the situation and gird on my armor for
another upset of family life. At least, I thought, we will be in
the new house and not have to be squeezed into the sardine
box any longer. I could not visualize another baby in that small
house. The rectory was nearly completed and I was asked
about the arrangement of shelves and drawers, and allowed to
choose the wall papers, quite as if it were my house. It was a
novel sensation for one who had been at the mercy of other
people's arrangements, and I hailed it as a bright spot in my
itinerant life but had to keep reminding myself that it was not
my house and I mustn't get too fond of it. It was good to be
with my husband again, we had seen so little of each other.
Moving was not hard this time. I took a good many things
myself in the baby carriage, going down a path through the
meadow. The little girls loaded up their possessions in the
express cart and thought it fun to move them. Of course Teddy

had to be toted every time and had a grand time getting into mischief. He was two in October and Marjorie four, their birthdays three days apart.

It was such a nice large, clean house, had a bathroom and furnace and even an extra room downstairs for a nursery. I laid myself out to have a pretty parlor again, and it did look really "refined," as the doctor's wife said when she came in. The dining room had corner cupboards for my nice china, and that was a joy. The study was nice and roomy and light. At last the parson had a place large enough for his desk and books. The nursery opened into the kitchen and was such a comfort, for visitors never needed to come in there and I did not have to keep it tidy. We had the big couch there, a round table, toy cupboards, my sewing machine, a canary in a cage and a little later a big square piano, sent up from New London when Grandpa Peck went to live there on retiring. That was wonderful for the girls and they at once began to learn to play. I could teach them a little and they were having singing lessons in the public school, which they now attended, to their great grief at first, but which they grew to like. They pasted bits of paper on the keys with the letters on them and worked away till they could play simple tunes. I helped them as much as I had time for, and when the piano and sewing machine got to going and the canary singing at the top of his voice and babies babbling there was some racket, but I did not mind, so long as they were happy. It really seemed as if I might live like other folks now for a while.

In the fall, when everything was in place, Theo invited the Archdeaconry to meet there and asked Bishop Williams to come and dedicate the house. This was the first Church function for me in a long time and I felt it was a pretty big thing to get ready for, and to have my family on exhibition to the officials for the first time. There was much fixing up of best clothes, which had had so little use of late, and making the house look as attractive as possible. Mary came on to help me and she was a host in herself, as always. We had plenty of flowers sent in for decorations, and the people of the mission sent good things to eat. I made great bowls of chicken salad and there were cold meats and beautiful rolls and cakes. Pears and grapes were ripe and made nice decorations. All the Church people and some of the neighbors were invited, and after their service in the church, the clergy arrived in full force and the house was well filled.

The children were nicely dressed and their hair curled and looked very sweet. All the visitors admired them and remarked on their bright faces. Baby boy was good and made no bad breaks. I think probably some of the clergy were surprised to see what a family the missionary had, and very likely shook their heads over it. The ladies, as usual, were charmed with Teddy's smile.

We had a fine luncheon and then the Bishop had a short service of dedication, and said how important it was that the mission should have a home for its minister and he hoped the work would now become permanent. Bishop Williams spent the night with us as we actually had a guest room now, and I was glad to have him sit at our table and see Theodore's family. He was getting old and was soon to have a Coadjutor. He was pleased with everything and it really seemed as if some progress had been made.

That winter they began talking about building a new church, selling the old, dark one and building in a better neighborhood where the people lived, instead of being crowded in between warehouses. This was not accomplished for several years but it kept the parson busy raising money. Also the people of Putnam were feeling the need of a hospital, as there were many accidents on the railroad and in the factories, and no hospital within reach. Dr. Morrell asked Theo to be on the committee to raise money, as he knew the rich people of Pomfret, so that was another piece of work.

Then too, his brother William had bought land in Pomfret for a school of his own and had become owner of one of the old Grovener boarding house buildings as a beginning and wanted Theo's advice and needed to see him often, so he was away a great deal and I saw very little of him. Our grocer man, a member of our mission, said that if they wanted money, all they had to do was to let Mr. Peck harness up the old horse and drive off somewhere and he would come back with it. He really had developed a gift for approaching people the right way and he also made a business of speaking for Eastern Connecticut in the different churches, especially at Archdeaconry meetings and was successful in rousing their interest and so raised a good deal of money that way.

Theo thought he ought to have more leg exercise, so he bought a bicycle and tried to ride it to Pomfret. It took him a good while to learn and he had a good many tumbles. One day the children came running in and exclaimed, "Oh, Mama, Papa has run into a wagon and is lying in the road." I rushed out and found him picking himself up unhurt, but it was not very safe for him with his poor sight to be on the public road. He would come flying around the turn into our place and land headfirst in the ash pile. Many times the children would come in shouting, "Oh, Mama, Papa's in the ash pile again." He finally got expert enough to ride it to Pomfret, though I was always on pins and needles till he returned.

And here comes in an incident which has been a family joke ever since. His brother handed over a good many clothes to him, knowing his necessities, and one time there came to him two sets of flannel pajamas. This was a new article of apparel to us, as they had just come into fashion, and Theo always preferred the old fashioned night shirt, so when he saw a fine striped brown and white flannel suit, he thought it was a summer outing suit, just right for bicycle riding. It was warm

weather just then so he put it on and rode proudly up to
Pomfret School and greeted his brother gaily. Will looked at
him in astonishment and then burst into peals of laughter.

"Great Scott, Theo, what are you doing riding a wheel in
my pajamas?" Aunt Harriet laughed too but Theo was
profoundly shocked. The poor innocent did not know what
they were laughing at until it was explained to him and then, of
course, he was much crestfallen. He explained that he thought
it was a nice outing suit, but saw the joke on himself and
laughed with them. Will never forgot the joke and passed it on
to all the members of the family, so poor Dad never heard the
last of it. His nature was so happy, he never got mad over
unimportant things, would always see the joke on himself,
even when his poor eyesight let him to do unexpected things.
He would exclaim "Great Scott" or "Jupiter Ammon" or
"contwist it," a substitute for "confound it." He did not even
say "darn it" except on very special provocation – I remember
once he fell down right in front of a lady, and got up and
laughed. She thought he was the most remarkable man she
ever knew.

I had many anxious evenings in Putnam for he insisted on
going downtown alone if there was a meeting to attend or he
had to see some parishioner who was only home in the
evening. He took his cane and held it straight out so he could
tap the trees along the edge of the sidewalk and know how far
he was from the gutter. He often fell down a bank or bumped
into a tree, knocking off his glasses or bumping his poor nose,
which got so many blows I used to wonder it ever looked
decently. He had to cross four tracks down by the station to get
into town and often engines were sitting there, blowing off
steam and he said the noise made him absolutely blind. There
were gates, though how he knew when they were down I don't
know. It kept me worried, but he never got run over and said
that being born on the Angels' Day he thought they looked

after him, he had so many narrow escapes.

The new house brought me great enjoyment, though not freedom from troubles. Lest this should be too much a catalogue of woes and troubles, I want to speak of our happy home life, the father being so much the center of good cheer that it was hard to have him away so much. When we were faced by some new difficulty he would say, "Oh, don't worry, let's laugh." He taught the children to see the funny side of hard times, and we would often sit down and have a laugh before the complication was straightened out.

We always kept the home festivals, birthdays as well as Christmas, and also the wedding anniversaries. He planned to be home if possible and would say to the children, "Look, this is the way we pranced up the aisle" and he would take my arm and show them the stately wedding march. We all had on our best clothes and sang songs and had a nice supper, with a wedding cake, always white with cocoanut frosting. There was always a little party for birthdays, with a cake and candles and presents no matter how small they had to be.

Thanksgivings were home days and we never accepted invitations out. I remember a well-to-do lady in Pomfret asked us to dinner as a great favor, but did not ask the children, and was surprised that I refused, and said I could not think of leaving the family on Thanksgiving Day.

Christmas was, of course, the great day and, sick or well, we always had the stockings and tree and home fun as well as the Church festival. The cousins, Jean and Harold, thought it the height of happiness to spend Christmas at the Pecks. As Harold said, "There's always something doing at that house."

In looking back I see that I was sometimes too much absorbed in the family and perhaps did not try hard enough to reach out and make more friends, but the fact was, in no place so far had there been more than two or three people I could really care for personally. They were pleasant acquaintances but not intimate friends. It was a day of rejoicing when one of my sisters or in-laws, or my friend Alice Knight could come for a visit and we could laugh and carry on and I could be young again. I fear I was not by nature social enough to make a large circle of friends, and the few I cared for were too far away to be of much use, so I had to get my pleasure with my children.

I remember our being shut in by a blizzard one Valentine's Day, Daddy away, and I shut in with the youngsters. I played games with them and baked some little heart-shaped cakes with pink frosting and wrote a poem for each child, and they decorated the table and we had a good time together.

When I see mothers now who leave their children entirely to nursemaids and are always out, seeming only glad to be rid of their brood, I'm thankful I was poor enough and lonely enough to enjoy living with my children. Theo enjoyed them too and liked to be with them when he was home. Nan remembers how she went to Church with him when I could not go and, because she was so timid, he let her sit in the chancel in one of the prayer desks, so she could be near him. It may have surprised the congregation to see a small girl sitting in a high-backed chair in the chancel, but she was not very visible to the people and felt the comfort of being near Papa. He sometimes took one of them on his Sunday trips, especially when he could spend the night at Grandpa Peck's house in New London, where he had moved after retiring.

I have a distinct memory of the first Christmas in the new house because we made one of those family excursions which were sometimes more pain than pleasure for me, although I did enjoy them too. Will had settled in a house of his own in Pomfret and Harriet asked us to come over and have dinner with them and join them in a tree for the children. I was to bring my presents for them and we would unite and have a fine tree.

I labored to get the children properly dressed, for Harriet's eye was critical. I remember how proud I felt of Marnie in a red coat and hood trimmed with fur, made over from one of Esther's. Little Ted, two years old, was very cunning in a coat and hood of grey eiderdown trimmed with swans down, made by myself. He looked like a little wooly bear. We went over on the noon train, after church, carrying much baggage and Will met us at the station with his carriage. We had a fine dinner with beautifully decorated table, turkey and all the vegetables, plum pudding for the elders, and ice cream for the children, candy and nuts. Ester and little Margaret were glad to see their cousins and the tree was lovely. They all sat around it while their names were called and then played with the new things. I remember that Nan and Esther had dolls with patterns for clothes, to teach them to sew, and that Alice was disappointed because she had something else herself. I had the misfortune to fall on the waxed floor with Teddy in my arms, which gave me quite a jar and made us all anxious about the baby to come, but no harm came of it.

In the early evening we had a bite of supper and then I packed up all the presents and things to go home. Jean Peck was with us, I have just remembered, and I have heard her laugh about this excursion. Teddy was tired, and excited at being out after dark, and as we drove along the dark road, he kept calling out "B'ars in the treetops" as he looked up at the trees waving over his head, or he would burst out with mixed up lines of the Christmas carols we had sung – "Ring out the bells Chris tree, happy day" or "Gaddy round Chris tree."

The train was an hour late and we had to wait in the small station. Ted got hold of my satchel and trotted round and round the coal stove, wailing, "Chu chu cars all gone away." Then he would climb up on the bench and look hopefully out of the window, then climb down and go on with his dismal chant, "Chu chu cars all - gone – away."

At last the train came and we got aboard. It was so late

when we got to Putnam that all the station carriages had gone and we had to walk. It was nearly a mile to the house and the wind was very cold. We plodded wearily along, Theo carrying Teddy over his shoulder, I leading Marnie, the girls loaded down with bags and bundles. Nan's hat blew off and she had to put down her baggage and chase it. The procession was demoralized, and when Marnie remarked, "I hope the bull dogs are all asleep" we nearly had hysterics at the picture of the procession being chased by bull dogs. We were just tired enough to go into fits of laughter.

We struggled along home and found the furnace fire was nearly out and the house cold. On the back porch was a freezer of ice cream, left by a friend as a present. It did not appeal to us just then. I made some hot cocoa and got the tribe to bed, weary but happy. I was glad to crawl in myself, for my bones ached. I thought, it's a good deal of a pleasure "exertion", though I had a good time too.

The date for my fifth baby was the last of March and I was getting ready all winter. I painted the family cradle white to make it last once more and bought a new baby basket trimmed with blue, and some kind lady in Pomfret sent me a most beautiful outfit, such dainty dresses, jackets and wrappers, and a wonderful soft blanket. They were so dainty that I thought the baby surely ought to be a girl, but it was destined otherwise.

I had not been very well and early in March I was taken sick with some kind of stomach disorder and lay abed two weeks, living on milk and a little broth. I worried about the baby but the doctor said it was living on my fat and would be all right. I grew thin, of course, and had no strength and I felt a good deal worried. We had no maid just then; they usually left if anything went wrong, and Mrs. Brown had to come in by the day. The girls were good at looking after the little ones, but Teddy would not leave me and was quite offended when the doctor would not let him sprawl on my bed. I remember him lying on the floor, close to the bed, a little bunch like a rabbit, in a pink pinafore, his face hidden in his hands. He could not be persuaded to leave "Mama".

Mrs. Gardiner came over one day to offer her help and found things so upset she insisted on staying all night. I did not want her to for I knew how messy things were and I was afraid she could not find a clean sheet for her bed. She looked around and found a ragged one, and had a chance to take note of our impoverished condition. The children were shy and Teddy would not let her put him to bed. She said Marjorie was the only one who was friendly. I suppose they looked upon her as an intruder.

Soon after this we received a large box of household linen from the Pomfret Auxiliary, which rather hurt my pride but was a great help. I had not yet become used to accepting charity for necessities, but as we went on I was glad to welcome it. We had hardly anything to spare for house furnishings and very little for clothes. We lived mostly on hand-me-downs, and went without extras. I had been so long without a new hat that I began to feel ashamed. I tried to put it out of my mind but the longing for something pretty took possession of me. I'm sure you girls will appreciate that as you probably went through the same experience in the course of our poverty stricken days. I got up my courage to tell Theo I needed a new hat and he said "Why, of course, go buy one, it won't cost much."

I had some money in my pocket which was supposed to last for quite a while. The minute I got into the millinery store my eyes fastened on a perfect love of a bonnet, white straw trimmed with narrow velvet ribbon, velvet ties under the chin and in front a most beautiful bunch of violets. I felt it was exactly the thing for me, it satisfied my longing for beauty and I must have it. When I inquired the price my heart fell, for it was five dollars, a fabulous sum to my economically trained mind, and I knew I ought not to buy it, but after trying it on, and being convinced by the milliner as well as by the looking glass, that it was exactly the right thing for me, I yielded to temptation and took the five dollars out of my purse, trying not to see how little was left for baby's shoes and other necessaries, and went home with my prize.

I had a guilty conscience however, and in spite of the little girls' admiration and rejoicing to see Mama in a new hat, I dreaded to tell Theo what I paid for it. He admired it and said how becoming it was, especially the violets, and then I confessed the awful amount I paid for it. His face fell but he said nothing. I said "I'll take it right back if you want me to" but he said "No, keep it. You don't often have anything pretty." So I kept it and after a while I lost my sense of guilt when I wore it. I recount this so you may realize how little we had that was not really necessary, but I did adore that bonnet and wore it a long time. In my elderly mind's eye, those violets are still beautiful.

This hat episode is a digression. The next important event in the sequence of this narrative is the birth of the last baby in this Peck family. He came along all right on March 30 in a wretched rain and snow storm the day before Easter. Theo was at home fortunately and I could get the doctor at the usual early hour and Miss Heath a little later. Doctor Morrell wanted to go to Providence on the seven o'clock train and kept looking at his watch to see if I would let him off. I was very accommodating and was through with him in time to let him catch the train. I had more pains than usual as the baby's head was large, but got through quickly and welcomed number five, a little brother for Teddy, two and a half years younger. He was fair and blue-eyed and while I had not been so crazy to have him I felt the same thrill of love and motherhood when I held him tight in my arms. I did not regain my strength as well as usual, and had a long weakness and was obliged to have treatments on the bed. Dr. Morrell said "No more babies, your organs are worn out." I was glad to agree that this should be the last, although both our mothers had eight children. I knew I could not keep up the family record.

All the relatives insisted that the baby should be called William for his grandfather Peck, and while I admired Grandfather greatly and would be glad to honor his memory, I did not like the name William, for I thought it too common and I knew he would be called Bill, which I disliked very much. I see now that I was all wrong in my feeling, for our first ancestor in America was William Peck and I should have been proud to continue the name, but sometimes mothers have prejudices, and I had my share. He got the name however, so my lack of proper feeling did no harm. I insisted on choosing his middle name and said it should be Laurence, because I liked the name. When we afterwards had a Laurence in the family whom we did not much admire, I didn't take much pleasure in the name. I was overruled about calling him by his middle name, and got used to the nicknames, Willie, Billy and Bill.

He was baptized on St. John's Day in June, and Welles Partridge acted as Godfather, Aunt Julia as Godmother. None of my children's sponsors amounted to much, and we soon lost sight of them, but fortunately their parents were able to look after them.

William was a sweet looking little fellow, as dainty as a girl with fair hair and very blue eyes, like his grandfather. He was not always sweet tempered, however, and had a strong will of his own and a loud yell. When I had him dressed up in the dainty clothes sent me, he looked like a girl and I took him next door to visit the elderly ladies who lived there. They thought he was adorable, and also loved small Ted who spent much time over there, carrying on his usual enchantments with the ladies.

I found the summer trying, with five children to look after and the baby's food to fuss with. I could not nurse him long and was not strong. Brother Will was so sorry for me that he proposed to finance a vacation for us. He said there was a small hotel at Webster Lake, Massachusetts where we could be comfortable and I could have rest from housework. This was most kind of him and the youngsters were overjoyed at the prospect of going away and living in a hotel. I had some forebodings as to how much rest I would get and wished I could take a nurse with me, but that was out of the question.

This lake had an Indian name about a yard long, which I will not try to write. The children spent much time drilling their tongues to pronounce it. Dad hired a wagon large enough to transport the family and the baby carriage, and Jenny pulled the load rather unwillingly and slowly.

We found our quarters very small, one room for me and the two babies and one very small one for the three girls. Nan and Alice shared a bed and Marnie had a cot. Teddy had to sleep with me and there was a crib for the baby. When Daddy came he had to lie on the floor with his feet up on the rounds of a chair because there wasn't room enough to stretch out. He didn't try to come very often.

It was very hot weather and the beds were made of feathers. There were thunder showers at night and one night there was an alarm of fire which waked us all up and the children were much excited when the fire engine came to a nearby house and a crowd gathered. There was no sleep that night.

I had an alcohol lamp to heat the baby's food and I had to go down two flights of stairs to the basement to get his milk and also to wash his diapers, so it was harder work than at home. The children had a fine time through the day, but it was work for me. I would start the procession for the lake soon

after breakfast, the girls carrying books, paints and playthings
for Teddy, I pushing the baby carriage, Teddy and Marjorie
stumbling along after us. We would dispose ourselves on the
beach and spend the morning there, all paddling in the water
except the baby, and I mending stockings or getting a peep at a
book now and then. Then at noon I would push the carriage
back up the hill in the blazing sun, my face purple with the
exertion, the children red as lobsters and bitten with mosquitoes. The ladies sitting on the piazza in their thin dresses,
rocking and keeping cool, looked at me with pitying eyes, and
no doubt wondered what in the world made me come there
with such a tribe of children. One of them actually put the
question to me, and I had to admit that I thought I was to have
a vacation and it was a change from cooking anyway. I know I
had their sympathy.

The meals were good in an old fashioned country way,
much corn, blackberries and huckleberry pie. One of the girls
had to stay on the piazza with the baby while the rest of us had
dinner. Nan and Alice took turns at it. Little Ted would march
into the dining room ahead of time, climb up into his high
chair and give his order. The maids thought he was too cute for
anything. The girls were much disgusted with a young man
who ate his corn with both elbows on the table and gobbled it.
They called him Mr. Hog.

Teddy, as usual, charmed the ladies. While they played
croquet he would stand and watch them, his wise little smile
ready for anyone who spoke to him. He wore a red plaid kilt, I
remember, as boys at that period were not put into trousers at
three years old. He had a white blouse and black velvet jacket,
and I thought it a very fine costume, though I did make it
myself. His sailor hat was pushed back on his head and his
brown curls were bobbing. The ladies thought he was too
cunning for anything. They were also surprised at the way he
and Marnie responded to my bedtime call. They thought it so

remarkable that the children came when they were called without any protest; knowing the discomforts that awaited them upstairs, I too, thought they were pretty good.

It was while we were there that I made my last attempt at painting. There was a lovely sketch I wanted to make and I sat up on the stone wall and with my oil paints on the palette tried to get it. But Teddy climbed up beside me and tried to help by sticking his fingers in the paint, all three girls had to have sketch books and try to sketch, the baby in the carriage fretted and wanted to "go", so I gave it up as a bad job and decided to put away my palette and hand over my artistic desires to my young descendants.

To cap the climax of this vacation, I took the family on a Sunday excursion, in spite of the fact that we had always disapproved of those things. A small steam launch took parties for a sail around the lake on Sunday afternoons and the girls begged to go. I hesitated because of the baby as well as my conscience, but finally consented and we got aboard with a motley crew of people, and were squeezed in between fat ladies and rowdy men, and my heart failed me as to how it would come out.

At first the children thought it fine, but when a thunder shower came up and we could not keep dry, and the sail was longer than we thought, they all got hungry, the baby cried, and Marjorie and Teddy were so restless I could hardly restrain them, so we arrived home late, tired and hungry, and I thought it served me right for going on a Sunday excursion.

We went home that week and Mama felt almost as tired as when she went away, and was glad to get back to her own airy rooms and have room enough to stretch out without being crowded. The children had a fine time and it was really a good change in spite of discomforts. At any rate, it made me appreciate home, as visits often do.

Up to this time I had been too much occupied with the

family to do any Church work, except to sometimes take a
Sunday School class or to be a substitute at the organ. It had to
be pumped with the feet, so it was not good for me to do it
often. Now that the children were older and I managed to keep
a low-priced maid, at least part of the time, it became
necessary for me to take some share in the doings of the
mission.

Theodore was elected Archdeacon of New London when
Mr. Jarvis resigned. This meant he had charge of two counties,
Windham and New London, and had to look after the aided
parishes as well as the missions, supply their services if they
were vacant, help out with their expenses and sometimes settle
their quarrels. This increased his work very much and he was
at home only one Sunday in the month. The Putnam people
were insisting on services every Sunday, so Theo arranged to
have the seniors at Berkeley Divinity School, Middletown, take
turns in coming to Putnam on Saturday night and conducting
services on Sunday. This meant that I would have to entertain
the young man, show him the way to church and explain
everything that he was expected to do. It proved to be something of a trial before the winter was over. The student would
arrive Saturday evening just as I was giving the little boys their
bath before supper. I would have to leave them in the tub and
sometimes Billy would escape and come running through the
hall, wet and naked, just as I was showing the young man to
his room. They had to get used to seeing strange sights in that
rectory. Sunday came to be a laborious day for me, and I
appreciated how ministers feel on Monday morning.

After getting the family dressed and fed, I would leave one
of the girls home to watch the youngsters and walk the mile to
church with the young man, show him everything, sometimes
play the organ and teach Sunday School, introduce him to the
people and walk home with him, then get the dinner and wait
on the family, with a high chair on each side of me and a

troublesome baby to watch while he learned to feed himself. I thought it only fair that the young man should carve, as my hands were so full, so I always put him at the end of the table and presented him with a carving knife. Some of the boys looked daggers at me and I know they didn't like it, but I thought it would not hurt them to have a little training in family life.

I remember Charlie Clark struggling with a "shoulder of ham," as we called it, and getting redder and redder in the face. I heard afterwards that he told his mother that Mrs. Peck made him carve and he thought it was very mean. I imagine the others shared his feelings though they were more good-natured about it.

I had a good deal of interest in studying the different young men and picking out those I thought most likely to succeed. I was right about one of them anyway, for William Jepson, a young man who was working his way through Berkeley by running the cafeteria, turned out to be very successful and built up a mission in Bridgeport to a strong parish, became secretary of Convention and made a name for himself. I saw that he was thoroughly interested in his work and not so fussy about surroundings as some of them. He picked out those people who needed visiting and gave his time to them as far as he could.

Then there was Welles Partridge, always a queer genius, Eddie Newton, destined for Alaska, little Weed, whom the other boys called the Venerable Bede, Bishop Atwill's son, who I think is now a bishop himself, and Laurence Shermer, he of the handsome face and beautiful voice who married into our family and proved very disappointing. Charlie Clark had a swelled head and put on airs. The boys laughed at him because he called himself the rector of Putnam; I used to get out of patience with him because he had to mail two letters to his girl the twenty four hours he was in Putnam.

One of them, whose name I have forgotten, boasted that he had never made a fire in his life, and I said to myself, if not to him, "Young man, I hope you will be sent to Alaska or the wild west, where you will have to take care of yourself and learn something." I have an idea they thought I bossed them too much, and I heard from the family in New London that I was said to be running the mission, which was certainly a new business for me, but I was really responsible, so I had to look after the embryo clergy, and learned a good deal. I would like to know what they said about me when they got away. They must have seen I had my hands full with those two small boys, Billy a holy terror. He was dreadful at the table, spilled everything around, and one day he threw a chicken bone which he had been sucking, right across the table and it hit Charlie Clark in the face. I was shocked, of course, but could hardly help laughing too at the expression on his face, which got redder than ever. His dignity was much offended and he could not see the joke.

One Sunday night when the maid was out (if we had one), I made a nice dish of milk toast for supper and was carrying it to the table, nice and hot, when the dish, which had been mended, parted company and crashed to the floor, spilling toast all over the rug. Funny how those little happenings stick in the memory all these years.

The young man always left right after supper to get the evening train and I was glad to see him go. I had to teach the small ones their Sunday lessons in the afternoon and read stories to them and I had no time to rest. After they were in bed I sometimes sat down to read and get a little mental refreshment for myself, but invariably fell asleep in my chair.

In connection with the children's lessons, I will recount an incident which impressed me a good deal. Marjorie, six, was learning the catechism and I was hearing her recite the creed while Teddy, aged four, was building block houses with his baby brother. After the lesson I went into the next room to read a little and I heard this conversation: Teddy, in a low, hushed voice, said, "Baby, what do you think?" Baby gave a grunt and Teddy went on, "Baby, what do you spose? Jesus went up to Heaven and sat down on God's....Hand." He said this with a curious mixture of awe and amusement in his voice, and then they both chuckled and went on with their building. I thought, that just shows what pictures form in a child's mind when we teach them these doctrines.

Theo came home between Sundays and looked after things in Putnam. The plans for a new church had been made and the old one was soon to be sold. Also the hospital fund was growing and in the course of a year they had raised money enough to start the work in an old house, by adding on some wings. It was called the Windham County Infirmary and could take five or six persons. Then later on they succeeded in persuading a Mrs. Kimball in Pomfret to give a large sum for the endowment of a hospital to be called the Day Kimball Hospital, in memory of her son who had died. It was completed in the course of a year or so and stood on high ground across the river from the town and became a very useful institution. Theodore served on the Board the first year.

Then a great blow fell. Theo's beloved brother William, head of the family and support of his old father, died suddenly of pneumonia. Pomfret School was making good progress and he was devoted to the boys. An epidemic of pneumonia caused a number of them to be ill and in his anxiety for them he stayed up nights to watch them, took the disease and in three days he was gone. The poor father was nearly crushed. He said, "I never expected to outlive him." He and the daughters were living in a small house in New London, which Will rented for them after Father retired from active work. Julia and Marion were teaching school and Clara was the house keeper. Will's death left them badly off and made a burden of care for

Theodore. His work in the Archdeaconry increased all the time and he was hardly home at all.

It was about this time that his eyesight became so bad that he went to Hartford to see his old oculist and was told that he would be entirely blind in about fifteen years. This was a hard outlook with such a young family, but we had to face it and Theo began taking out insurance and trying to lay up something in the bank, but it was hard to spare anything from the daily expenses. That was one of the times when our faith was tested, but he was so brave and cheerful about it that I had to try and be cheerful too. As it turned out, he was able to see enough to keep on with his work until the children were grown up and had left home and he could see partially for a few years more. This shows how useless it is to worry about future troubles. When Theo consulted another oculist, when he had to get a certificate for his retirement pension, this doctor said that no doctor had a right to make such a positive statement, it might have had a very unfortunate effect. I want you children to realize how courageous your father was, to carry that burden of dread all those years and not let it depress him. The poor eyesight was a "thorn in the flesh" and was always getting him into embarrassing situations, but he buried his aggravated feelings and went cheerfully on. In case any of you don't know what the trouble was, I will say that it is called "retinitis pigmentosa," the gradual formation of pigment on the retina, which, of course, cannot be operated on and which obscures the light more and more until total blindness results. It is easier to bear than sudden blindness, as one can be training the sense of feeling and laying up memories of just how things look, before the sight gets too dim. That doctor gave him fifteen years, but it was nearer thirty before the final darkness fell. He could have left you no better legacy than that spirit of faith and cheerful courage which carried him through all the hard times and enabled him to do a very useful work in spite of handicaps. This disease was inherited from his grandfather and is said to run out in the third generation. It has never shown in his children.

Colchester was one of the places he had to help fill, as they had no rector for a while, and one Saturday when he was over there he walked across the green where the boys were playing baseball and a ball hit him in the abdomen so hard that he fell down and had to be carried to his boarding house next to the church. The doctor being summoned, said that it was a bad bruise and he would have to lie abed a week at least. There was no service that Sunday. He wired me to come right over and take care of him and I took the baby and started right off, having telegraphed to sister Mary to come and stay with the family. It was her vacation and I knew she would.

I found my poor man most uncomfortable in his cheap boarding house. It was hot July weather and he lay on a feather bed, that being the only kind in the house. The landlady's daughter, a fat, shapeless young woman, rather infantile, had a crush on the minister and insisted on nursing him. He told me he sent for me to save him from her, as he disliked her attentions extremely. She was jealous of me and there was an undeclared war between us, I using every strategy to keep her out of the room, and she sulky and offended when I got in ahead of her.

This was my first experience of a cheap, country boarding house and I was truly amazed at the table they set, no nice ordinary meals, everything greasy and badly cooked. I went down to breakfast the first morning, having been awake most of the night suffering with the heat, and beheld a table spread with ham and eggs, bacon, pancakes, muffins, doughnuts, bananas, pie and even layer cake. What little appetite I had fled at the sight, and worst of all was the coffee, the traditional boarding house coffee, like dish water. When Theo first came there he had asked if he might have cereal, and they did make oatmeal after a fashion, and I tried to eat that.

The Fourth of July was extremely hot and I got a bad headache. We were both famishing for a cup of good coffee and when one of the nice women of the parish came in to ask if we were comfortable, I ventured to tell her of our troubles, and she insisted on smuggling in a good pot of coffee with sugar and cups, and we had a nice private picnic and enjoyed it. The friend also insisted on loaning a mattress, as the doctor said it was bad for the poor man to lie on feathers in the heat.

I had my hands full with the nursing, keeping Bella in her place without offending her, and looking after Billy. He was at the running away stage and as soon as let out would go flying down the sidewalk and I would have to give chase, not knowing how far he would go or where he would stop. I tried putting him inside the wire fence in the back yard, but he upset the chickens' water and chased the hens so hard they had no time to lay eggs. The mistress complained and I had to keep him upstairs with me. I could sometimes keep him quiet by giving him a large sheet of paper and telling him to make letters. He would cover the sheet with strange characters and shout "Big I.D." He thought he was making letters. He had to sleep with me and was so restless that I got very little sleep and of course he climbed on the bed and bothered his Daddy, so I decided to take him home. A note at the bank was due and had to be renewed, so I went home with the little rascal and consigned him to Mary, telling Nan and Alice they must help chase him and keep him out of mischief. Theo began to get well of his bruise and after another week I brought him home and he was able to take up part of his work. This was the first time he had been knocked out of his work and he was much disgusted. Usually he got over a cold very quickly, or any little upset. Dr. Morrell said he was like a rubber ball – you could not keep him down.

In the fall of that year a great change came in our family

life, a very hard one for me to face, though nobody at the time knew how hard, for I kept it to myself and did not want anyone looking on and criticizing. Theo's father had been very ill in May and they thought he would not live. His children were all with him at his bedside, expecting the end, when suddenly he revived and began to recover. I was interested in Marion's remark: "He had his children all with him, his work was done and it was the proper time for him to die. It would have saved complications." Of course they were all devoted to him but I understood what she meant.

His recovery did make complications, for he could not pay the rent now that Will was gone. It was before the day of the Church pension and he had only a small stipend from the infirm clergy fund and some gifts from old friends. Julia and Marion were self-supporting and the family decided it was best for Father and Clara to live with us and pay a small sum which would cover their food. They all said Clara would be a great help to me and of course Father was a perfect saint and would be a blessing to any family. Of course I knew all this was true and yet I felt I wanted my home to myself. My husband was away so much, I had all the care and discipline of the children and did not want anyone looking on and criticizing. Clara and I had been friends since girlhood and the children were fond of her. She was a perfect saint, but one of the unselfish people who sacrifice themselves with a martyr spirit. I knew that martyr expression so well and that she would have plenty of opportunity to put it on. She had a way of getting her feelings hurt at something and saying nothing but going around with that martyr expression on, which was very irritating to me, as I did not know what was the matter. I had to wrestle with my feelings considerably and remind myself of my promise, "Thy people shall be my people." Theo never knew that I was not perfectly willing and I would not confess it now if there were any chance of its getting to Clara's ears, but she, poor dear, is past being worried by it and the saintly father is in his long home, so I may as well make a clean breast of it. Since those days Dad and I have come to be in the same position, Grandparents living in a family of young children, and perhaps Alice can appreciate my feelings at that long ago time.

Father had a weak heart and had to be carefully watched, and Clara insisted on staying with him day and night, so we gave up the guest room to them and she had a cot at the foot of the bed. They moved up most of their furnishings and their room was so full they could hardly move. The looks of my "refined" parlor were changed entirely when their stuffed furniture was moved in and I had to make room for many precious family treasures which must be kept. It did not look like me anymore, if you know what I mean. Kitchen furnishings also filled the cupboards, and in the attic drawers and boxes were full of things that must be kept.

Father was a wonderful man, a real saint, but I felt he was annoyed at the children's naughtiness and quarrelsomeness. The boys were at a trying age, especially Billy, and when he kicked and screamed at the table and had to be carried out, I felt that Father was critical of my management. Billy was a holy terror just then anyway, climbing up on everything and falling down, trying to come down the stairs head first, and continually getting bumps and bruises. I came in one day and found him dancing on the dining table, brandishing a carving knife and bowing to himself in the mirror.

Teddy admired his tall grandfather very much and liked to walk with him, trying to make his small steps keep up with Grandfather's long stride. Both boys loved him and would run in to kiss him goodnight, sometimes before their faces were washed and I would see him wipe off their buttery kisses. Clara was a help with the work and often stayed with the youngsters when I had to go out.

Our home of course became the headquarters for the

family, an embryo Rooftree, you see, and when Julia and Marion came up for vacation, it was a little hard to find room for them as the guest room was given up, but we managed to find a corner somewhere. They were there for Thanksgiving Day and I stayed home from Church to get everything ready for the large dinner party. Teddy was feeling sick – said his throat was sore – and I knew I ought to put him to bed, but could not stop work long enough. He sat around, watching me, heaving sighs and saying "Oh dear," but he wanted to come to the table and try to eat a little. After dinner he sat in Aunt Clara's lap and went to sleep and I knew by his heavy breathing that he was sick. I got him to bed and used the remedies we had on hand for sore throat and in the morning called the doctor. He pronounced it a bad case of tonsillitis and said he must be isolated. Julia and Marion thought best to go home Saturday and that relieved my care somewhat. The doctor thought on Saturday that Ted was no worse, but that night I felt very anxious. Theodore had gone to his Sunday work, and Grandpa was to read the service in Putnam, as he was still well enough for that. Sunday morning I asked him to stop at Dr. Morrell's on the way to church and send him out, but Doctor was already out on his rounds, so I could not get him till afternoon. You people with telephones don't know what it is to have to wait so long for a doctor. When he came he looked very grave and said he wished I had called him sooner, it was membranous croup and very serious. I held the light for him to look in the throat and saw that the tonsils almost touched, hardly a hair's breadth between them, and the hoarse breathing was in the wind pipe. Doctor said it would be an all-night siege, and how I did wish for my husband, but there was no way to get him home before morning. Doctor came twice that evening and at nine o'clock brought a tank of oxygen and showed me how to handle it. He said it was only to be used if the child got cyanosed. I know he hated to leave me alone but there was no nurse in town and Clara had to be with her father, so I prepared to sit out the night alone. The doctor wrote out the directions for treatment, something every twenty minutes, and said I was to call him if I got alarmed, but how could I except by sending out a child or old grandfather in the night?

That was the longest night I ever spent, sitting close to the bed, giving the treatments, watching for the dreaded blueness in my boy's face. He was so good, lifting his head or opening his mouth when I asked him to, making no fuss and holding my hand all the time.

Towards morning his breathing grew easier and at day light I felt sure I would not have to use the oxygen. Doctor Morrell came early and brought Doctor Overlook of Pomfret, also surgical instruments, to perform an operation on the wind pipe, but they found it would not be necessary. He congratulated me on my treatment and said he felt that we would be all right now.

Theo was to come home at about eleven that morning and I watched for him. I heard his cheerful humming as he came down the sidewalk, swinging his bag, all unconscious of the tragedy that might have awaited him. He was shocked, of course, when I told him, but thankful it was no worse. He took right hold of the nursing and sent me to bed that night.

I dragged around for a day or two, feeling sicker all the time. My throat was sore, my bones ached and I lost every bit of appetite. The family got alarmed and called the doctor. He looked at my throat and said, "That's bad. You must go right to bed." It was diphtheritic throat from Teddy's germ. I didn't see how I could go to bed with Teddy so sick and Billy fretful and not well, but Doctor insisted, so Baby's crib was moved into the girls' room, where Marjorie was already stowed away. She and Teddy roomed together and of course she had to get out. There were four now, all bunched up in one room and the girlies felt that they might as well be in an orphan asylum or a hospital ward. Aunt Clara helped put Billy to bed, and we were getting quiet, when I heard a loud, hoarse bark, and my heart began turning somersaults. "Another case of membranous croup," I thought, and it was with great difficulty that I restrained myself from getting up. Theo brought the doctor and he calmed my fears, said it was only ordinary croup and would pass off. He gave Billy ipecac and showed the girls and Dad how to put hot compresses on his throat, and after awhile he got quiet. Doctor left, having told me not to get up under any circumstances. Dad watched over the whole lot of us and by morning Billy was all right.

It was agony for me to swallow and they kept me on milk and whiskey punch, and Theo had to swab my throat and nurse me and Teddy. By Saturday we were all better and he dared leave for his Sunday work. I reminded him again of my prophecy about the family being a mill stone around his neck.

By Christmas we were all fairly well and able to celebrate mildly, and we had our first missionary barrel. I had helped to send plenty of them but never had one before. Some large parish in the district had heard of the troubles in the mission-ary's family and had been working for us. There were bath-robes and knitted slippers for all the younger ones, nice clothes for the girls, toys and dolls and a large tea-set for Marnie – the joy of her heart, till Billy pulled off the table cover and broke a good many dishes, which nearly broke her heart.

In January Teddy began to complain that his knees hurt and he fell down often. Dr. Morrell thought it was rheumatism, but before long he got so that he could not stand up at all, if put on his feet he would sink right down. The doctor then said it was paralysis from the diphtheria poison but would pass off. He had earache too, and lost his hearing entirely. We had to shout to make him hear. He was awake nights with earache and lost every bit of appetite. I remember his little pale face on the pillow as we tried to coax him to eat, and his weary but determined voice as he said, "I don't want anything to eat."

We had to keep him on liquid peptonoids, beef extract, etc. Every morning I had to put him in a bath of sea salt and then rub him all over with cod liver oil. Then I would put on his flannel nightgown and wrapper and carry him down to the nursery, where he sat all day on the couch with his playthings, or rested on the pillows. He was good natured and patient, which was a blessing, as Billy was enough to keep one person busy. He had a running ear and sore finger and seemed to have some poison in his blood, and was so cross and nervous it was hard to live with him. He was cutting double teeth and was wakeful all night and was so tired of his bed he made me get up at dawn and hold him while he played with the "little min," as he called the chess men and other games. I was a perfect slave to him, I know, and I can just picture myself, sitting there, nodding with sleepiness and holding that squirming little imp in my lap. I had to battle with him every morning to get him dressed. As soon as I tried to slip his shirt over his head, he would fly into fits of rage and tear it off. I would put him in the crib and tell him he could stay there till he was a good boy. He would run to the edge of the crib and try to throw himself over, with such a wild look in his eyes I felt afraid his brain was giving out. He was just a little bundle of nerves and as soon as I touched him he would go into spasms. If I left him he would go into a frenzy. So the battle of the shirt went on and we were both exhausted by the time he gave in and was dressed.

I asked Dr. Morrell to come and look him over, and after hearing the tale of the shirt, he said, "I suppose you don't dare spank him?" I said, "No, I really don't, he acts so wild, I fear his brain is affected." He said, "Well then, we'll have to put him on bromide." He fixed some medicine in a glass and told me to give him a spoonful every three hours and more at bed time. It worked pretty well, he slept much better that night and woke up good-natured. I approached the shirt act with fear and trembling, but to my surprise he listened to the funny story I was telling (a device often tried but never successful before) and let me put the shirt over his head with only a few squirms. When Doctor Morrell came in later in the day, I pointed to an angelic, golden-haired infant, trotting smilingly around the room and said, "Behold, a reformed character. Blessed be bromide!"

So the winter passed with me doing nothing much but nursing, no church-going or recreation. I was thankful there were no lay readers to look out for. Father Peck was able to read service and one of his own sermons and that saved having anyone from outside.

When spring came Teddy was able to walk a little and his hearing gradually came back. Billy became more civilized, though he was always a kind of tempest in a tea-pot. On a nice sunny day I asked the doctor if they might go outdoors and he said, "Yes, but for heaven's sake, don't let them get wet!"

I wanted to have Teddy's picture taken before his curls were cut off. They were in a sadly tangled condition during his illness. Dr. Morrell used to laughingly threaten to bring a lawn mower and cut his hair, but I patiently brushed and combed them out, little by little, until they were smooth and shiny, and I made his first trousers. He had been wearing kilts so far with white blouses. I made a small pair of pants and an open jacket from a discarded blue serge dress skirt, and a blouse with ruffled collar, a la Little Lord Fauntleroy, who was all the rage just then. I had his picture taken and then his hair was cut and he was a real boy.

The new church was under way now, the old one sold and the congregation moved into a disused Unitarian building. This was most unattractive, dark and gloomy, no chancel, just a high platform, a cabinet organ down below and the choir in the front seats. The altar and other church furnishings had been moved in but did not look at home. It was in this unsatisfactory place that Bishop Brewster, who had been made Coadjutor to Bishop Williams, made his first visit, and Nan and Alice were confirmed. There were no white dresses, veils, flowers or candles, just ordinary clothes and a plain service. I was sorry they could not have a brighter place to make them feel at home in their Church life.

We were just getting acquainted with Bishop Brewster who was to be our very dear friend in the days to come. Putnam was a railroad junction and sometimes the Bishop would have to change cars there and wait, so he would run out to the rectory and eat supper with us very informally, just our plain supper of cereal, bread and butter and baked apples or gingerbread. We were afraid the young hopeful, Billy, would say something rude. He had been playing with chess men, and for some reason of his own called the bishops, "biting Bish." We were in terror that he would get off that remark, but for once he kept quiet. After the Bishop left, he and Teddy said with broad grins, "Bishop Brewster ate a rooster," but we let that pass.

Father Peck was getting more feeble and the people felt they needed a resident minister who could give them his whole time, so a strange man was invited to come and live in Putnam, but was told he would have to rent a house for himself. This was only a brief interlude, and I introduce it just to show what some clergymen are like, though I hope not many. This man came well-recommended, but we were disappointed when we saw him. His name was Dr. Hall; (how he managed to get a degree I don't see). He was stout and florid, wore a silk hat well pushed back, and went around with a big, black cigar in his mouth. He was very familiar with the working people and told such stories and jokes around town that the nicer people were quite offended. I disliked him intensely and I know Grandfather did, though he would not show it. He still kept his seat in the "chancel" and the contrast between his saintly face and Dr. Hall's red visage was striking. This man tried to change everything, choir included, and insisted on playing the organ himself. He would open the service, then step down and play the organ most vigorously, singing the Venite in a mighty voice which drowned out the feeble choir, then up the stairs to read the lessons, down again for the Jubilate, up again for the Creed and down for the hymn. Poor father looked quite distressed and the young people were much amused.

Good Friday Theodore happened to be home and there were the three clergymen in the chancel (so to speak). The Pecks supposed of course Dr. Hall would preach, as he was in charge, but when it came time for the sermon he announced that they wouldn't have any sermon today, and he left the church hastily, his cigar already lighted, to get the paper and hear about the ball game. That finished him for us, and Theo found, on talking with the people, that he was doing more harm than good, so he found a way to remove him and we went back to our old ways.

Father kept on reading service till Laurence Shermer was ordained deacon and put in charge of the Putnam mission. He rented a room near the rectory and so began the romance which brought him into our family.

When summer vacation came, Julia and Marion came to us as usual. George Peck also came up to see his father and celebrate the Fourth. It was extremely hot and on Sunday the third, Julia was overcome in church. She was standing by me, singing the Te Deum, and suddenly sat down. Clara saw that she was ill and went out with her, and in the vestibule she collapsed and became unconscious. George also went out and got the carriage (Jenny was standing in the horse shed), and they took her home. We had a cot on the verandah for the warm weather, in the shade of the vines, and they put her on that. When the rest of us got home, she was lying with one eye open and one shut, breathing hoarsely. When the doctor came he said it was not sun stroke, but apoplexy, probably a hemorrhage on the brain. He said she must not be moved to the hospital, but he got a nurse from there and they moved her on the cot to the parlor and took out most of the furniture. The doctor said she must stay right there and be kept absolutely quiet.

The next day was just as hot and the children were disappointed that they could not have firecrackers in the yard. They were sent off with their crackers and something to eat, to a neighbor's yard and told to keep away from the house.

Dr. Morrell brought a brain specialist who happened to be summering in the neighborhood and they had a consultation while we anxiously awaited the verdict. The great doctor said it was a hemorrhage on the brain and gave it as his opinion that she could not live, but that if she did by any chance survive, she would be a hopeless idiot. He told that in plain, unvarnished language to the poor father, and I thought he was brutal.

The nurse sat by Julia all day, her fingers on the pulse, and every little while she thought it had stopped. Julia was unable to swallow so they stopped the medicine but gave shots in the arm frequently. Theo sat there too, watching, with his prayer book open at the prayers for the dying, he felt so sure she was passing away. Towards the end of the afternoon the nurse felt a slight increase in the pulse and tried putting a spoonful of medicine to the patient's lips. She swallowed, and in a few minutes the pulse definitely improved. They called the doctor and he said he saw signs of her coming to life. They gave strong injections and by bedtime the doctor announced that a miracle had happened and she would live, but it would be a long time before she regained consciousness and her life depended on absolute quiet.

You can imagine my dismay. How impossible, I thought, to live that way all summer, those noisy little boys, Billy at the roaring age, bawling and having tantrums frequently, the dining room right next the sick room. They put up a sign to keep people from driving into the yard, and said to keep the children in the back rooms. I fed the children in the kitchen and tried to decide what to do. I remember almost choking Billy, to stop his noise when he went to bed, and running down stairs to get a piece of gingerbread to bribe him with. Whenever he yelled, the nurse would come up and say, "This noise must stop. It is disturbing the patient."

When I got them all to bed I went to Theo in his study and said to him, "Something must be done. I'll be a raving maniac if I have to spend the summer this way. It's impossible to keep the children quiet and Julia's life depends on my doing it. We must do something – what shall it be?"

Theo pondered awhile and then said, "Yes, we must do something. I'll begin looking around for a place where you and the boys can go and stay awhile. Meanwhile, suppose we ask our good neighbor, Mrs. Allen on the corner, if she can let us use one of her bedrooms at night, and let one of the girls sleep over there with Billy. Teddy can be kept quiet, perhaps." This suggestion was followed and for a few nights the small boy was put out of his home, but he was very unhappy and when he came home and got in my lap and begged to stay, I felt it was cruel to send him away. His head was hot and I knew he was not well, so I put him to bed upstairs and he kept quiet for once. Next morning Theo and I set off in the buggy with the boys and Marnie and a suitcase, to find a place of refuge. Theo thought perhaps Judge Catlin, who had a large country place in Woodstock, and who was a bachelor with no family but a housekeeper, might take us in. His mother had been a good friend of ours before she died, and the Judge was a member of the Putnam church. He was naturally surprised at such a request, but had sympathy for us, and said he would ask his housekeeper. Of course we offered to pay board, and he said he would not take it, except that he would have to pay her something extra. The good woman was evidently not much inclined to take on such a family, but finally consented and I promised to take care of our rooms and help her in every way possible. Theo left us and we settled ourselves for a real country visit. There was plenty of room for the children to roam without getting into mischief and Marjorie was a good guardian for the boys always. Theo rode out on his bicycle to see us and tell me the news. You must remember we still had no telephone and I felt cut off from my world. He reported that Clara and the nurse were running everything and the colored maid was docile and indifferent to what happened. We stayed there a week or so and then the housekeeper thought she had had enough of it and we went back home to see how things were. Julia was showing slight signs of regaining consciousness but it was just as necessary for her to be kept quiet.

Our next move was to the Pomfret rectory, as the Gardiners were going on a vacation and said we might have the house for two weeks. We took all the girls this time and I drove Jenny back and forth while Theo was away, to bring our washing home and get things we needed. I felt like an exile and it was strange to go home and find other people running my house.

They even seemed to wish I wouldn't come at all. Then in August, light broke on our perplexities. One of the rich friends in Pomfret heard of the troubles and sent Clara a sum of money, I think two hundred dollars, to use in some way for Julia's comfort. Clara said they did not need it, as other friends had offered to pay the nurse, and she wished I would take the money and get a cottage at the shore for the family until September. She said that would help Julia and all of them more than anything else. I had to agree, of course, and through a New London friend we had the offer of a cottage at Pleasure Beach, near New London.

The children, of course, were delighted to be at the

seashore, and I was glad to relax and try to come down from the high nervous tension at which I had been living. The children could play safely on the beach with their sisters to watch them, and I could lie in the hammock and rest, no work but to get meals.

While resting down there I had a chance to hear from Nan and Alice something of what was going on at home. They said Aunt Clara was running everything and was jealous of the nurse and wanted to take care of Julia herself as she had always been the family nurse, but Miss Holmes was very firm in keeping her own place as head nurse. They said Aunt Marion was having a good time with Mr. Shermer, going to ride with him as Dad had left Jenny and the buggy at home, and the perspicacious Nan was sure something was going to happen in that direction. Thirteen year old Alice kept her own counsel and did not reveal even to her sister's sharp eyes that she was desperately in love with the young minister herself and was cherishing the thought that he would wait for her to grow up and marry him, and she was frightfully jealous of his attentions to Aunt Marion. The young man had a fatal charm of looks and manner and was so affectionate with Alice, thinking of her only as a sweet little girl, that her young heart fluttered in her breast, but she kept her secret hidden. She says she used to wait after evening service to walk home with Mr. Shermer, but Aunt Marion and Aunt Clara were always in the way. I would I had the pen of a novelist to depict the romance of this period, but I will have to just record the facts and leave some other writer to work it out.

When September came and school time drew near, we began to think of home. Now that the days were shorter and we had no good light for the long evenings, we began to long for our own house. Theo came down one day and said that Julia had improved so much that the doctor said it would be safe to move her to another house. They found one on a street

near us which could be rented, and were planning to set up a
home of their own again. So many friends had offered to help
that they felt sure of being able to pay the rent. The young
parson would take a room in their house and that would help
the expense. "Oh yes," I said to myself, "I see exactly what is
going to happen." He said Clara was busy clearing out her
possessions and we could have our home to ourselves again.
He also said that he felt quite sure Laurence and Marion would
be married eventually and would want to live in the rectory,
and that we would move to Black Hall. The shore missions
were demanding more attention and the Bishop wanted him to
make that his headquarters. I went home with mingled
feelings, so glad to have our home to ourselves and yet with the
shadow of another move hanging over me.

We found a dilapidated-looking house when we got home.
Clara had snatched out everything belonging to them and had
not stopped to put things to rights. The dining room rug and
sideboard had been taken and the parlor denuded of everything, having been a sick room all summer. Drawers and
cupboards were halfway emptied and everything in confusion.
The fierce joy which Clara showed in taking possession of her
things showed that she had missed her home more than we
knew, and was as glad as I was that the change could be
made. How we women do hang on to our own place and our
own things!

Julia had been carried through the streets on her cot and
was not conscious of having been moved. She now had her
eyes open and was able to say a few words, but her hands were
helpless and she only moved a very little, and did not recognize
anyone.

We went to work to get settled at home again, fill the empty
places and make things look as they used to. The children
began school and we let Marjorie start now. She was not as
terrified as her sisters had been and liked to go, but she soon

got over-tired, for they pushed her ahead too fast, because the grade was full and younger children must come in. They put her in long division before she had learned the multiplication tables, which of course was disastrous. She brought her work home and I had to help her every night. She worried and worried and before spring she began to have twitching eyes and face, symptoms of St. Vitus dance, and we took her out of school.

I soon saw that an engagement announcement was inevitable and I could not feel happy about it, for Marion was seven years older than Laurence, and while so fair and young-looking with her yellow hair and blue eyes, she had never been well since a long illness with spinal trouble in her girlhood, and I feared for her future. The young man had developed traits which made Theodore fear he would not be a success in the ministry. He had a beautiful voice and could read and speak most attractively, but he was determined to have his own way, was ready to flout the authority of the Church and did not take kindly to being directed. He had a large idea of what the Church owed him instead of thinking what he owed the Church.

Marion had always been the fine lady of the family with extravagant tastes, and had been rather selfish about getting more than her share of the good things which were none too common in the Peck family. Theo and I, knowing what sacrifices the ministerial life demands, felt afraid they were not cut out for that kind of a life.

I had not been home long when I realized that the young man had cast his glamour over Clara also, always acting so affectionate as if she were the most desirable woman in the world. I suppose he had the fatal gift of wanting to please everyone and showing feelings which he did not really possess. He certainly must have had unusual powers of attraction to gain the affections of a little girl and two women older than himself, all in one lump. Marion was the chosen one and I have never doubted that he sincerely loved her, but it was too bad of him to act so affectionate with Clara. Perhaps he did not realize that her feeling for him was more than a sisterly or even motherly affection. I think Father wanted Clara to have him because he knew how lonely she would be when he had to leave her and how much she needed someone to love and look after. All her life she had had someone depending on her for care.

A few weeks after we got home Marion came to Theo and me and revealed her happy secret – no secret to us – and we had to congratulate her and wish her happiness, though we felt so dubious about it. Theo felt she was not fit to undertake the duties of a clergyman's wife, but he could not tell her so. His mother had made him promise, as Marion's guardian, that he would not allow her to marry without a doctor's certificate, which shows that Mother also had her doubts about the wisdom of marriage for Marion. Theo insisted on her going to New London and seeing a doctor who knew something about her and he gave her permission to marry. That relieved Theodore of responsibility but he still felt that her previous history showed too many weaknesses to be able to endure hardships. The sequel showed he was right and in after years he had much anxiety and distress about his "little sister."

Alice was told the news and she concealed her heart ache and her tears in private. She says she kept hoping something would happen to Aunt Marion, and Laurence would wait for her to grow up. How tragic is a young girl's first love! Clara too had to express pleasure, but she wore a hurt look and did not give up pampering Laurence, in spite of Marion's disapproval.

Laurence now had a room in Grandpa Peck's house and his relations with both women became very intimate. Marion often complained to me about Clara's absorption of Laurence and said he did not like it but was afraid of hurting Clara if he objected. She said Laurence never dared kiss her good night unless he kissed Clara first, and that Clara insisted on waiting on him, sitting up nights to make him a hot drink if he were late, and even getting up in her kimono to play checkers with him if he could not sleep. Marion was torn with jealousy all the time but would not let Clara know it.

I also had my feelings hurt. I had been teaching in Sunday School and singing in the choir and I suppose showing more interest in the conduct of the mission than I ought to, owing to my previous responsibility, and Laurence did not like it, thought I was trying to manage and interfere with him. I had been in the habit of buying the presents for the Sunday School Christmas, and without thinking, began making plans for it, and Clara told me plainly that Laurence and she would see to that, so I was squelched, and thought it time to resign all my positions, which I did very soon and there were no regrets expressed. I realized I was not wanted anymore and that my day in Putnam was over.

On Christmas Day Father was in church for the last time. He had taken cold but insisted on going just the same. He pronounced the benediction after the Communion Service and I thought as I looked at his saintly, peaceful face that it was like the face of an angel. That night he was taken with pneumonia and it was hopeless from the first. Julia's nurse was still there but Clara shut everyone out and devoted herself to her father. I know how her heart was rent with grief and did not blame her. Marion and Laurence had not told him of their engagement, I suppose because they knew how he felt about Clara, and Marion told me that the last morning of his life they stood together at the foot of his bed with their arms around each other, to let him know, and she said his dying eyes looked at them with an expression of dismay and then turned to Clara, as if to say "She is the one." Marion understood and it rankled in her memory for a long time.

About this time Julia came to herself, was able to get up
and walk with the nurse's help, and her mind was perfectly
clear. To Clara's great dismay, she announced that she was
going back to New London and live with her friend Alice Bush
as before. This was another blow for poor Clara, for she had
taken for granted Julia would live with her, and now that
Father was gone she needed her so much, but Julia was firm
and they had to give their consent. She went back and
gradually recovered enough to help herself somewhat, though
her hands were unsteady and she walked very slowly. Her
mind was perfectly clear and when her eyes had been attended
to, she could read and occupy herself. Her mind was just as
fine as ever and she was always a welcome guest in her
brothers' homes. So much for the prophecy of a crack specialist
that she would be an idiot!

The new church was now ready and June was to be the
time of its opening. Laurence was to be ordained to the
priesthood in June also, and after that their wedding would be
in the new church. That made a good deal to look forward to
and we were all very busy.

Marion, in addition to getting her trousseau ready, was
embroidering a beautiful white stole for Laurence and he was
helping her, as oddly enough he had a gift for needle work. He
said his mother taught him. They were sitting up nights over it
and this displeased Theodore as he thought Laurence should
have been studying for his examinations. He was a good deal
dissatisfied with the young man already and dreaded having
Bishop Brewster's keen eyes look him over.

The ordination was in Norwich and Theo went down to
present the candidate. Laurence had to be examined by the
Bishop the night before and made a woeful failure of one
subject. Theo knew why and did not like to look at the handsome stole. Bishop Brewster was much disturbed at Laurence's
failure and told Theo he really ought not to ordain him. He

seemed to comprehend the young man's outlook and his lack of fitness. He told Laurence he must study with Mr. Peck and make up the subject he had failed, but Laurence was too cocky to do this and we left so soon that Theo could not insist.

One reason for Laurence's lack of success was the adoration he received from both Marion and Clara. They would never acknowledge that he could do anything wrong or make a mistake. Such double adulation was enough to spoil a man of that type. Bishop Brewster never liked or trusted him, and for that reason Clara would have nothing to do with Bishop Brewster.

Next on the program was the opening of the new church, and soon after that the wedding. Marion was insisting on a fine, orthodox church wedding, though some people thought she ought not to make so much fuss, not being a young girl, and having lost her father, and Clara being on the verge of exhaustion. The general opinion was that she ought to be satisfied with a plain wedding, but after all, it was the rector who was getting married and Marion had been saving her money while teaching and could pay the expenses herself. I did not blame her for wanting a lovely wedding, her romantic soul was wrapped up in it and she planned all the slightest touches to make it an unforgettable event. She said that her three nieces, Esther, Nan and Alice, should be bridesmaids, and she would furnish the dresses and have them made by a dress-maker. This was a generous offer and a relief to me, of course. So Marion purchased fine white lawn and the girls were fitted to their fluffy dresses, much tucked and trimmed, and were quite excited at having to go to a dressmaker for the first time in their lives. They were to have pink sashes and white Leghorn hats trimmed with ribbon and pink roses. Alice had to bury her hurt feelings and find consolation in the new finery.

I also was busy with clothes, contriving something for

myself to wear – I have forgotten what – making a white dress for Marnie and white pique suits for the little boys. Billy was quite well behaved now and looked sweet when dressed up, with his pink cheeks, blue eyes and yellow hair. Ted was so cute too in his white suit, with his brown curls, short but still charming. Marjorie was to wear white with blue ribbons, and of course new shoes had to be had all around, so it was quite expensive.

George Peck came up to give the bride away, and was so impressed with the importance of his duties that he borrowed a silk hat, frock coat and cane, and got off the train in great style, to the amazement of his brother who met him. We tried to laugh him out of it and persuade him to wear plain dress, but no, he was going to adorn the first wedding of a Peck sister with proper costume. We couldn't help but laugh at old George, the insurance agent, so rigged out, but he enjoyed himself hugely.

The June day dawned clear and hot and we all went to the church. I sat in the front pew with Marjorie and the boys, all looking very sweet, the boys like cherubs with their white suits and shining locks. The bride came in, her dress of white silk with long train and her face like marble under the tulle veil. The tenseness of her feelings had taken every bit of color from her face. The girl bridesmaids looked very sweet under the wide hat brims and the nodding pink roses. Laurence's brother had come from Philadelphia to be best man. Theodore married them and Laurence had insisted on having the Communion Service there and then, so it was a long strain for the girlies, kneeling on the chancel floor without support. The little boys got to wriggling a good deal but I managed to keep them down. Laurence's mother sat opposite me and wept profusely all through the service. The boys eyed her with wonder. Billy whispered, "What's she crying for?" Perhaps she also felt a doubt about the suitability of the marriage.

After the service we all went to the Peck house where Clara had prepared a luncheon and then off went the newlyweds to enjoy a short vacation and we were left to clear up the mess. Poor Clara was on the verge of exhaustion and after dragging around a few days, the doctor made her go the hospital to rest and have treatment for her spine.

As for me, I was desperately tired and I turned to the weary task of getting ready to move once more. We had already packed a good deal but the last things had to be done and the house cleaned for the newcomers. I felt somewhat as if I were being put out, but of course Theo's work was demanding the change, and through his efforts the Putnam Mission was now on its feet and under Laurence's charge.

The family at Black Hall. Top row: Bill, Anna, Theo,
Front: Alice, Marjorie, Anne, Ted

Bill, Ted, Marjorie, Alice, Anne Peck

Theo at his desk

Anna Elizabeth Abbott Peck

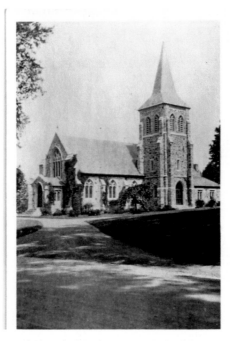

St. John's Episcopal Church, Washington, CT, built under the leadership
of Rev. Theodore Mount Peck, completed in 1918

The Rooftree in Washington, CT, across the street from St. John's Church,
where Theo and Anna lived with daughter Alice and her children after his
retirement. Also this is where the book was written by Anna with Alice,
during the 1940s, likely based on Anna's diaries and letters to her mother.

Abbott home in Waterbury where Anna grew up.

The Merriman house in Watertown, CT, as described in the book, the farm where Anna's grandparents lived, and where she visited as a child.

Life in Black Hall 1896-1902

I now come to the next chapter of our history, our life in Black Hall, but before I take up the narrative I want to give you a picture of the place as I saw it and see if it agrees with your own memories.

You children should really be writing this chapter, for you came to Black Hall with joy and enthusiasm and found it an adventure in country living and new experiences, whereas I came very tired, looking forward to hard work with few conveniences and a rather lonely life, except for the family. There would be no society, no really congenial friends, nothing inspiring except nature and not even a church. I had been shut in with the family illnesses in Putnam and I was getting rather fagged out with seven years of missionary life, and longed for something more settled and a chance to improve my mind. The children were older now and would not fill my life so completely as before. However, I girded up my loins once more and determined to try and look on the bright side, if possible.

Black Hall was a tiny little village at the mouth of the Connecticut River, opposite the Saybrook light. It was named, they say, for a black man who built the first shack there in Colonial times. A creek wound through the salt marshes to the river and the tide rose and fell in it.

The Black Hall school for boys was the principal interest in the village, founded and owned by Charles Bartlett. His wife, Mrs. Annie Bartlett was a remarkable woman and both she and Mr. Bartlett had done a fine missionary work in the surrounding country among the poor people and had been responsible for the building of the Guild Room mission, a plain building which provided a place for Sunday services and also weekday entertainments. Theodore had been making visits there and holding services while we were in Pomfret and Putnam.

Mrs. Bartlett had died the year before we moved there, which was a great loss to me, as she would have been a wonderful friend.

The Lane family, descendants of early colonial settlers, lived on Griswold's beach right on the Sound, about a mile from the village. They were well to do people and very good to us, letting us use their beach and bath houses, and were helpful in the mission.

Aside from these few I had met no other people except the two De Wolf families, one of the men being the postmaster and the other a farmer across the street from our house. Their wives became good, kind neighbors.

Now I must describe the house we were to live in, a fine old white house, square and comfortable looking, a typical Manse, we thought, so we called it that. It had been the home of a sea captain named Falls, who had left it to his sister and she in her will had left it to the church as a minister's house. We were the first minister's family to live in it.

The house stood on high ground on the road to Lyme, under great elm and cherry trees, and looked solid and comfortable. At the side was a rough lawn ending in a sloping cliff with ailanthus trees and sumac bushes growing out of its crevices. It was a fine playground for children. There was a square porch over the front door and a paved path led to a white gate in a picket fence. On either side of the path were tall Spanish Bayonets which blossomed in summer and also laburnum trees which in spring shook out their yellow tassels. There were many flowering shrubs in the front yard and when I went down there in May with Theo to look at the place they were all in blossom, a very sweet front yard.

On the other side of the house was a garden plot with an asparagus bed and an orchard full of peach, pear and apple trees, and beyond that a meadow full of grass with daisies and buttercups.

There was an addition built on for the kitchen and a long tail of sheds running behind it, including a summer kitchen and a shop used by the captain for carpenter work and mending shoes. A ladder led to a loft overhead and that was a wonderful place to explore. There was no barn, just a shed where Jenny could stand, but no box stall to lie down in.

There was a fine outlook over green fields and blue water, and the mingled scent of salt marshes and upturned soil in spring was delightful. Jerry said it made her understand the meaning of "salt of the earth" – she was sure it was that smell. There was always the sea view, calm in the sunshine or wild in the storm, a few sails moving and, at night, the lights of the steamers creeping along the horizon. The Saybrook light shone out at the mouth of the river. There was always a fascination about looking off the sea.

Back of our place was a high hill scattered over with boulders. It looked as if a giant had shaken them out of his apron. Small cedar trees grew here and there and a brook ran down, tumbling over the stones in waterfalls. This was Meeting House Hill, probably the site of the first settlement, though there was no sign of a building.

There was quite a bit of land belonging to the property, fields where rye and oats could be raised, and the parson's soul rejoiced at the thought of having a "glebe," real land of his own to use. He had inherited a love of the soil from his English ancestors and his greatest desire had always been to own a piece of land. This, to be sure, was not his own, but he could have the pleasure of using it and "pretending" that it was his. As his jurisdiction was now confined to the shoreline, he would be at home more and have time to work on the land.

You can see what a pleasant prospect it was for the family, a summer by the sea, trips to the beach for swimming, fascinating places to explore. The neighborhood of the Black

Hall School was an added attraction for the girls, just getting to the romantic age, boys to look at and perhaps get acquainted with. Marjorie and the boys were keen for adventure and could roam the country safely.

Now to take up the narrative again. As I related in the closing Putnam chapter, I was the last one to leave the rectory. Theo had driven Jenny down and the girls had gone to New Haven for a visit, and I was left with the two little boys and the canary bird to come by train. I had to hand over the keys to the honeymooners, and they were late getting back, so I could not take the morning train as scheduled. When we arrived at Black Hall station just at dark there was no one to meet us. Theodore had met the morning train and then had to go off somewhere so was late in coming to the evening train. We waited a few minutes and then the station master locked up and went away, so we climbed down the long flight of steps to the street and wandered along till we came to the Guild Room and sat down on the steps to wait. The boys were tired and their faces smeared with the chocolate they had eaten on the train. The canary wisely put his head under his wing and went to sleep.

I suppose there never was a more tired, homesick and forlorn creature than I was that night, as I sat in the twilight and looked around at the deserted street – no signs of life anywhere. It seemed a sorry welcome to a new home. The boys were getting fretful and impatient when finally Dad came hurrying along, so sorry to be late.

"I had to go away and could not get back in time. We are to stay at the Bartletts over night. Can you walk that far if I help you?"

"Yes, I guess so, but where is the trunk?"

"Oh, we can't get that tonight. There is no baggage delivery here. I'll have to come tomorrow with the wheelbarrow and get it."

Shades of my ancestors, I thought, what have I come to?

He supported me with his arm and we trudged along to the Bartletts' and found the family had finished supper and gone out for the evening. The housekeeper set a small meal for us, I don't remember what, except that there were prunes and I was ashamed to find that my tears were running down and mingling with the juice. I had gotten beyond self control and could not help it. I don't know what the housekeeper thought of such a forlorn, weeping minister's wife, but she looked at me rather coldly and I was glad the Bartletts were not at home.

I said to Theo, "Where are we to sleep?" and he replied "Teddy is to sleep with me on the third floor and Billy with you in the guest room." I unpacked the suitcase and found to my dismay that by some mental aberration I had put the nighties in the trunk. "Well, boys," I said, "you'll have to sleep in your underwear." "All right," said Teddy and marched cheerfully off upstairs, but Billy was indignant and waxed furious, protesting that he could not possibly go to bed without his night shirt. My arguments and persuasions were of no avail and he howled for half an hour, being as nervously upset as I was. Finally I remembered that there was still a piece of chocolate in the suitcase and I offered him that if he would stop crying. He consented to munch it between his sobs and crawled into bed where he was soon fast asleep. I longed to follow but had to wait for the family to come home and meet the new Mrs. Bartlett, which I dreaded. I lay down for a while, then washed my face and prepared to be respectable. The family arrived and I was introduced to them all. Mrs. Bartlett was very sweet and tried to make me feel at home, but I fear Theo was rather disappointed in me for once.

I got rested enough over night to feel some courage, and in the morning directly after breakfast we went over to the Manse. We found the kitchen piled with packing boxes right up to the ceiling, the cook stove sitting there, not in place, (imagine having to move a cook stove!), no furniture in place, no beds up, nothing unpacked. It looked like a hopeless task to get settled. I was gazing around, wondering where to begin when I heard a knock at the door, and there stood a round, fat Irish woman with a broad grin on her red face, who announced cheerfully, "I've coom to worruk."

Mrs. Bartlett had sent her. Her name was Ellen and she was such a welcome sight that I felt like falling on her fat neck, but did not. We all got to work and by night things were so far in order that we could cook our supper on the stove and rest our weary bones in our own beds. As I dropped off to sleep I thought "Be it never so humble, there's no place like your own, even in the midst of packing boxes."

The boys were perfectly happy, racing around, exploring everything, and thought it a great lark to eat off packing boxes and climb on all the piles. In fact, moving was always a picnic to the children. They had their night shirts and went to sleep peacefully.

We rose next morning with new courage. It was June, the bob-o-links and meadow larks were singing, the grass knee high in the yard, full of buttercups and daisies, blue sky and sunshine and the bracing salt air from the sea. Life looked more possible to me and Dad was singing for joy, getting ready to cut the grass and start the garden.

Gippy, the boys' pet tom cat, who had been shipped by express, arrived and was released from his cage, his face streaked with soot and what appeared to be tears. The boys were sure he had been crying and they petted him and fed him all the dainties they could lay hands on. His one eye looked at them affectionately and he soon became reconciled to his new home. Old Ellen was his friend from the first, and waited on him hand and foot. She kept a row of small dishes on the high in the kitchen, "little soops for Gippy," she said, and when he came home in the morning from his nightly prowl, she would shout in her jovial voice, "Gippy's landed. Do ye hear me? I say

Gippy's landed," and she would burst into loud "ha ha's" and proceed to rub him off with a towel and set all the "little soops" before him.

The girls arrived from New Haven and were full of joy at the prospect of country life, enthusiastic about all the beauties around us, especially the sea. "Oh, the salt!" they exclaimed, snuffing it with joy. They had to explore every corner of the house, led by the boys, who, as first arrivals felt like hosts. Up they went to the attic and down to the cellar and out behind the tails, finding all sorts of queer treasures hidden away, even a set of paper novels tucked under the eaves in the attic, old logbooks and journals of the sea captain, fascinating things. They discovered the sky light on the roof and poked their heads out of it, deciding at once that it was a fine place to get out and sit on the roof.

In the cellar was a large cistern which caught the rainwater from the roof, our water supply. The youngsters climbed up a ladder which rested against the cistern and looked in. Marjorie was ahead and came down in a hurry, almost knocking the boys over and they all rushed up the stairs shouting, "Oh, Mama, there's a skull floating in the cistern!" Horrified, I called Papa and we went down. He climbed up and looked into the cistern and came down laughing heartily. "They saw their own faces bobbing around in the water," he said, and we had a good laugh at the imaginative Marnie.

The girls began to plan out the rooms and of course I had my say too. There was a large room opening into the front hall, not connected with any other room. This was a real old-fashioned best parlor and had been carefully preserved. It had a white wall paper with gilt figures, quite antique and white paint entirely unmarred. There was a coal grate and a marble mantel. The whole style was Victorian, I suppose, but we modernized it soon enough, for in some mysterious manner we had been able to purchase in Putnam a Brussels carpet to cover

the entire room. Theo said it was necessary for the floor was
rough and cold and we needed to make the room look nice for
visitors. We also had a piano sent from home, my sister Kate's,
a maple upright in good condition and the girls were
delighted. The old square Peck piano had given out and been
disposed of. We put the best furniture and pictures in this big
room and felt we really had a "best parlor" at last.

At the end of the hall were two rooms opening together,
study and dining room. There were fireplaces and mantels in
both rooms and a high cupboard in the dining room for my old
china. We also had a present from Mary of a large black walnut
sideboard, which had been in her schoolhouse, but now the
school was given up and she had no place for large furniture.
This was grander than anything we ever had, with its marble
top and carved game birds over the mirror. We were glad we
had a large house for once, and felt quite like aristocrats.

The big kitchen was warm with the coal stove and a large
pump at the sink brought water from the cistern. Outside there
was a well for drinking water.

Upstairs the rooms were small and unheated. We had to
put up stoves in winter, except the boys' room, which was over
the kitchen and had some heat from the chimney. A steep
staircase led from the kitchen to the back ell where the boys
slept, and a continuation of it went on up to the attic so that as
I looked at it I had a vision of small boys, a clumsy maid, or
even a Mama falling down from the attic right to the kitchen,
but that catastrophe never happened.

We had no visitors that first summer and spent the time
getting acquainted with our new surroundings and our
neighbors. Some of them had funny names. The De Wolfs were
our nearest neighbors and the youngsters had to go there every
morning for milk. Mrs. De Wolf was very nice to them and
treated them to candy Sunday mornings. Jerry tells in her
story of Black Hall days how they used to look around the

room while Mrs. De Wolf was getting the milk and wonder where the candy was, then spy a paper bag on the mantel and fix their eyes longingly on it till she came in, then carefully look away and express great surprise and joy when she gave it to them.

The Bumps and Brambles lived nearby and the children named one house the "robin's nest" because Mrs. Robbins lived there and another the "jackdaw's nest" because of little Miss Dawes. They roamed and explored to their heart's content and we called them the Trio.

Marjorie, whose nickname was now Jerry instead of Marnie, was always the captain. She was full of imagination and could invent wonderful plays, and also had such good common sense that she could be trusted to bring the boys safely through their escapades. She trained them too, and when Billy refused to tie his shoe and demanded that she do it, she said no, he must do it himself. After trailing along a while and tripping over his shoestring he would give in and tie it himself. He was a stormy little tyke and would go into a tantrum if he got mad. Jerry tells how they settled their quarrels by pretending to fight duels with wooden swords painted on the tips with red paint. Billy sometimes got mad and made a really savage attack and then the other two would run away from him and scramble up the big cherry tree, which Billy was not yet able to climb, and there tantalize him by swinging on the branches and filling themselves with cherries while he battered the tree below and yelled. After a while he would give it up and settle down with a book to read aloud with a humming noise and they would slide down the tree and drop cherries in his lap and the fight was over.

I have often wondered since those days if Marjorie sometimes felt left out. She was the between one and the older girls felt rather above her and she was pushed off to the boys for company. She had commenced to write poetry and the sisters teased her about it, so she kept her writings locked up in her bureau drawer and wore the key around her neck. She was intensely alive to the beauties of nature and wrote about birds and flowers and brooks, and also kept a daily news record of the family doings – the colds and ailments, the number of eggs the hens laid and all the happenings. I regret now that I did not have more time to give her, she was such a dear, wise little companion and had such a wide awake, thoughtful mind. She was still having nervous twitching of face and eyes and was not allowed to read much. When she got tired her eyes would roll up and the boys would shout at her, "Stop dealin' up your eyes." The doctor said she would get over it if she lived outdoors, and that summer was a free and happy one, enjoying nature to the full.

The boys were a funny little pair, Ted philosophical and good-natured, already learning to help, bring wood, etc. His Godfather, Welles Partridge came down to see us and asked where the baby was. He was amazed to be told that his God child was chopping kindling!

Billy was hot tempered and sometimes so naughty that he was put on the cellar stairs where he kicked and battered the door and sometimes had to be taken out and spanked to make him behave.

Nan was very much the older sister now, turning up her hair and wanting her dresses lengthened, chiding the young ones for lack of manners. She was getting very particular about dress, clean hands and nice appearance and her small brothers could think of no more scornful epithet to hurl at her than "dainty!" which they did with great vigor. However, she was able to forget her dignity enough to sit on the ridge pole, ride Jenny bareback and sometimes play in the hay mow. She was showing great talent in art and was a great reader, devouring all the books she could find. Both she and Alice could play the piano, having taught themselves and worked away at it.

Alice was a real outdoor girl, enthusiastic about country life, but also romantic, looking at young men with adoring eyes, but secretly, never revealing her romantic dreams. She still liked her long braids but turned up her hair sometimes when she felt grown up.

The father was still strong and enthusiastic, glad to be at home more, though he still had long trips to make but could get home at night. He bought a two-seat wagon so we could all ride to the beach, and we had some nice afternoons that way when he was not too busy. The autos were just coming in to use and he insisted on one person riding backwards to watch out for them, knowing what would happen if Jenny got frightened. He raised fine vegetables in the garden and planted oats and rye in his fields. In the fall how proud he was when he reaped the rye and brought it home, later taking it to the mill to be ground into meal which made the most delicious muffins. Lady Jane profited by the oats and to pay for them the parson made her draw the hay which he cut in the yard, much to her disgust. She preferred to be a lady and have a man draw the hay, but he told her she had to work for her living.

I have been describing the family and must just add that Marjorie was such a very pretty little girl with her flaxen pigtails, very blue eyes and rosy cheeks, that one of the Old Lyme artists stopped her on the street one day and asked her if she were a little English girl. She said "Oh, no, American," but she showed her English descent plainly enough. The family were all good looking, in fact, and when the boys with their shining locks were sitting clean and demure in the front seat at service, some admirers told me they looked like little angels. I smiled and said nothing.

The only drawback to the summer was the mosquitoes, which were so thick and fierce that we could not sit out in the evening at all. They bit in the daytime too and devoured us if we worked in the garden. I had to put newspapers inside the children's stockings to keep their legs from being eaten up. The neighbors assured us that another summer we would be immune, so we lived in hopes.

We sat indoors evenings and I read to the three younger ones, Billy in my lap and Ted and Jerry on the floor close to my knees. We read the old favorites, *Alice in Wonderland, Swiss Family Robinson, Back of the North Wind, The Princess and Curdie*, and when a book was finished, they would say "read it again."

Ted did not want to learn to read but Billy was determined to, although I did not want him to learn so young because I knew he would be one of those children who have their nose in a book when they ought to be outdoors. He would learn in spite of us, spelling the words on the boxes when he rode on the grocer's wagon, and shouting out to be told what they were, spelling long columns of words in the dictionary, and demanding their meaning, till we gave up and let him learn. He soon began to read any kind of book and did it out loud with a droning sound like a hive of bees. One day he exclaimed, "Et tu Brute," and we knew he had been at Shakespeare.

Our orchard was a joy from the time of apple blossoms in the spring to the early summer apples and then the harvest of late apples, pears and peaches. It was a new experience to go out in the September mornings and find the grass full of pink peaches and pick up great pans full and then eat our fill. I put up many cans of fruit and preserves and in the fall Dad would take the children on trips to gather wild grapes, so good for jelly. We lived on the fruits of the earth and, although we at that period had heard nothing about vitamins, we absorbed them just the same.

Our Animals

We were all well-housed now except Jenny and she had only a shed, no place to lie down except when she was turned out in the orchard to disport herself, and then she ate too many green apples.

Dad had a scheme for getting a barn built and had put aside some small savings from his salary as a starter, and now he appealed to Burton Mansfield, treasurer of the missionary society of the Diocese, and asked him to come out and look over the situation. He came quite soon and we had a nice visit with him. He joked with the children and they thought he was great. They afterwards spoke of him as the Elephant Man, because he had such a large nose.

He surveyed Jenny's poor quarters and said he was sure a missionary horse who had travelled so many miles ought to have a better place to rest herself, and he would see to it that funds were voted to put up a barn. Theo insisted it must be a good barn, large enough to hold the hay he raised and to provide a stall for a cow, as well as a box stall for Jenny. After a little the order went out to build a barn in Black Hall, and Dad was told to engage the carpenters and superintend the work. This made him happy for he was now a real country parson and could pretend he owned property.

The men arrived and we older ones as well as the youngsters watched with interest while the frame was laid out to be fastened with great wooden pins. It was a real, old fashioned way of building, laying out the frame on the ground and then raising it with a large number of helpers. It was very exciting when the day came to raise it. All the carpenters in the neighborhood were invited to come and help, and we all held our breath when they pulled together and the great frame rose slowly up, the posts were set in their holes and there was the skeleton of a barn.

I had baked a large batch of cookies and the girls made
lemonade and the men stretched themselves on the grass while
we passed the refreshments. The children were much excited
at seeing a real, old fashioned barn raising!

In a few weeks the barn was finished and the mow filled
with hay. When Lady Jane was introduced to her fine box stall
with its carpet of clean straw, she lay right down with a snort of
satisfaction and rolled over with her legs in the air. We were
glad she could have a comfortable place, but sometimes she
was so provoking that we thought she did not deserve such
comfortable quarters. Sometimes on Sunday morning she
would get loose and go out in the orchard early and when Dad
was ready to start for his ten mile drive to South Lyme or still
further, to Niantic, and went to catch her, she would elude him
and gallop away, and he would have to pursue her till he was
all out of patience. Sometimes one of the girls would come out
with a lump of sugar and entice her into being caught, thus
rewarding wickedness. We thought she meant to make him
late to church, she was such an unregenerate missionary horse.

Once in Niantic when she thought the service was too long,
and it was dinner time, she untied herself somehow and went
grazing around the town and it took the parson so long to find
her that he was very late to dinner.

She had an uncanny faculty for getting loose and one
afternoon at the beach, while we were swimming she untied
herself from the hitching post and went exploring. When we
thought it time to go home, after eating supper on the beach,
Dad went to get her and she was nowhere to be seen. He
started out to find her, breathing out wrath, and she was
discovered halfway home, grazing by the roadside with the
wagon perched precariously on a high bank. He led her back
and we all got aboard. When she was out of temper after an
escapade of this kind, she would put her head down and run,
while we held on for dear life. We got out of patience with her

but she did work hard and carried the missionary many miles, so we could not begrudge her the new barn.

Dad now announced that it would be good economy to keep a cow. We had a good stall for her and pasture right on the place and he could raise partly enough hay for Jenny and the cow. The children were delighted at the prospect of another animal, and smacked their lips at the thought of cream for breakfast. I even suggested that we might make a little butter or sell a few quarts of milk. The family council agreed that it was a good plan, so the parson as he went on his visiting tours inspected the various barn yards and came home one day with the news that he had found a cow for sale at a great bargain and had agreed to buy her.

"Is she a yellow cow?" asked Jerry.

"No, she's a brown cow," said Dad, "big and bony, but she gives good milk, they say."

"Let's call her Buttercup," said Billy, "because she will give us butter and we can drink her milk out of cups."

We laughed at the flowery name and still more when the cow was brought into the yard, led by a man and accompanied by a dog. To quote Jerry, "We three stood in a row and watched her walk solemnly up the drive and felt a little disappointed that she was so big and ungainly, with high shoulder bones, as we called them. We had expected a pretty, gentle cow but this creature was not prepossessing. As she walked her toe bones clicked viciously and she had a way of shaking her horns which was quite disconcerting."

The parson was sure he could milk her as he learned to milk when he worked on a farm as a boy, but he found it wasn't so easy and sometimes Buttercup kicked over the pail or switched her tail in his face which was confusing, but he persisted and we had a large pail of milk every night and thick yellow cream for breakfast.

At the same time our pleasure was mingled with worry, for

the cow got to be quite a terror, she was so belligerent, and I began to think she wasn't so much of a bargain after all and had been sold to get rid of her. When we tried to cross the back yard where she was pastured, she would put down her head, shake her horns and come for us. Even the big girls fled screaming before her, and when I went to the well or woodpile I armed myself with a broom to keep her off. She chased Billy one day till he climbed to the top of the woodpile for safety and stayed there till someone came to rescue him. When any of us started for the rear, Dad would sing out "Keep your eyes peeled for Mooly." We always took weapons with us.

She sometimes got into the garden and laid it waste, and one day she stuck her head into the well to try and get a drink, her horns caught on the well curb and she pulled the whole thing off and ran wildly around, butting into everything, while we shrieked with laughter. Dad got a man to help and they succeeded in releasing her before she entirely smashed the curb. Aunt Julia was there and told the story to her New London friends, and they could hardly credit such a tale, a cow running around with a well curb on her head!

She capped the climax by getting into the orchard and making herself drunk on rotten apples. She got so sick that she had to lie down and could not get up. Dad got the cow doctor and he dissolved yeast in a long bottle of water and poured it down her throat. I was away somewhere and when I came in the boys ran to meet me, exclaiming, "Oh, Mama, the cow got drunk and lay down and couldn't get up and they gave her yeast and she rose!"

This spoiled her reputation entirely and she was sold at a loss and another cow purchased. This was a gentle, fawn-colored Jersey with mild eyes, who became the children's friend and let them pat and feed her from their hands. They named her Daisy and she gave many quarts of milk.

Our other animals were the cats and also some hens and a

rooster which were installed in Jenny's old coop, and gave the children much pleasure in feeding them and collecting the eggs.

I have told you how Gippy came by express and how old Ellen pampered him. She continued her morning shout of "Gipp's landed, I say, Gipp's landed," and one morning we heard an extra loud, "Ha, ha," and she shouted, "Gipp's landed – I say, Gippy's landed. Do you hear me? He's landed and brought a little lady with him." We hastened to see about it and sure enough, there he was with a small white cat with black spots, one of those cats who look as if their hair had been parted in the middle but just missed it. She looked to me like one of those old-fashioned china dolls with black parted hair. She had a meek little face and Gippy was certainly a gentleman for he stood by while she ate and touched nothing till she was through.

Of course we named her Lady and she became a member of the family. In due course of time she produced a litter of black and white kittens and as there was plenty of room and plenty of milk, we let them all live, to the children's great delight. Lady was a remarkable mother as well as a great hunter. She would come home early in the morning before even Ellen was up, leap to a window at the end of the shed, with a rat or rabbit in her mouth, run through the loft to the ladder, climb down, lay out her prey on the shop floor, slit it nicely and then call the kittens to breakfast. Sometimes she would make several trips and we would find a regular butcher's shop with the game all split and laid out. She was a hard worker and kept the mice and rats away.

Our Domestics

Old Ellen, as I have said, was our first helper and kept us laughing as well as properly fed. She was a great cook and

made all our bread, six great loaves twice a week, besides
brown bread and muffins, none too much, however, for the
hungry family. She also made pies and puddings, but not the
lighter desserts. When I came down in the morning she would
shout, "The top o' the world to ye, bizness is rushin'. Look at
me brid," and she would point with pride to the shining brown
loaves just out of the oven. She had not been taught about
cereals and said, "I don't know much about them combusti-
bles." I suppose she meant "comestibles," but she learned to
cook them and they did not blow up.

She stayed quite a while with us and then one day she came
to me with a sheepish look on her face and said in a solemn
voice, "I must go and see the world." I suspected from the look
in her eyes that she was 'hankerin' for the bottle, and I tried to
persuade her to stay, but she repeated that she must "go and
see the worrld." She promised to come back in a few days and
we waited hopefully but she did not come. Then some weeks
afterwards she appeared with a badly changed face and aspect,
looking completely demoralized, hair untidy and a frown on
her face instead of a smile, and said in a grumpy voice, "I've
coom fer me dudsies." I tried to find out what was wrong and
make her change her mind and be nice again, but talking was
of no avail and she waddled off, a short, round little Irish
woman with a bundle in each hand, and our cheerful Ellen was
no more. Afterwards, when Alice was at St. Margaret's, she
wrote a sketch for the school magazine entitled "Old Ellen,"
which took a prize.

We got along for a while without help except a woman in to
wash and clean, but I was not strong and there was much hard
work, carrying water upstairs, emptying slop pails, filling
lamps, and many things we did not have to do in Putnam. I did
not want to put too much on the girls, who were already
helping with the light work and making over their clothes. I
wanted them to have time to enjoy the country and their

sketching and reading, so we made up our minds to apply to
the employment bureau in New Haven and try our luck there.

It fell to Theodore's lot to be the martyr who would do the
interviewing, as I knew it would be altogether too much for
me, so he gritted his teeth and went in to New Haven. He
returned in the evening in an exhausted condition and we all
ran to meet him. "Did you get anyone?" I asked eagerly.

"I talked to every kind of a creature, black, white, and all
nationalities," said he, "and I got something. I don't know
whether it's a maid or the sister of the Queen of England, but
it's coming on the morning train." "Dear me," said I, "what
can she be?" He remarked, "I hope she'll stay at least one
night but I wouldn't be too sure."

We felt decided qualms as to what she might be, and
waited expectantly while Dad went to the train. He came back
escorting a fine lady, clothed in the latest fashion, with newly
curled hair and a condescending expression. I asked her name,
and she said it was Louise. Dad looked supremely disgusted
and whispered to me that she had brought an enormous
Saratoga trunk and he would have to bring it in the wheelbarrow.

"Well," I said, "it looks as if she means to stay awhile."

By the time he had wheeled the trunk home and boosted it
up two flights of stairs to the attic room he was red in the face
and wet with perspiration. He retired to the study to cool off
and I waited for Louise to change her dress and come down.
Presently she appeared in a light, starched print dress and a
white ruffled apron, and I was almost afraid to ask her to wash
the sink full of dishes that were waiting. I retired to the front
yard and compared impressions with the girls.

"She's quite a lady," said Nan. "We must have her wait on
the table and answer the doorbell."

Alice was shaking with laughter. "Do you really think she
can cook a beefsteak? And what will she say if we ask her to

carry the slop pails?"

"I must confess," said I, "that I don't expect her to stay more than one night."

Louise had to have a good deal of help about the dinner but was in her element when it came to waiting on table. She stepped mincingly around, carrying each plate out separately, even making an extra trip with each salt cellar, while the family wished she would step lively and bring the dessert. Our usual method was the hasty removal of dinner plates and the putting on of dessert without delay. The boys got out of patience and told Louise to hurry up with the pudding but she looked at them reproachfully and continued her slow and stately stepping about. When she had finally left the room the youngsters burst into merriment and we had to laugh too.

"Well," I said, "I'll be afraid to ask her to wash the clothes or scrub the floor."

"What do we want such a piece of china for?" said Alice.

Nan remarked, "It would be nice to live the way she's used to but I fear it wouldn't work here."

The boys and Jerry expressed their scorn, and Billy pronounced with a sniff, "She's dainty." which was the worst thing he could say.

"I know one thing," said Dad, "she'll give notice tomorrow and I'll have to lug that confounded trunk back to the station."

He was a true prophet, for next morning Louise came down with red nose and weeping eyes, and said, "I can't stay here, it's too lonesome in the country, it's so dark at night and I hear strange noises. I'm used to living with nice people and I can't do this hard, rough work."

I did not try to dissuade her and we washed the dishes while she put on her glad rags and bade us farewell, while poor Dad, sweating and puffing, wheeled the enormous trunk to the station and got some men to help boost it up the stairs to the platform. When he got back he relaxed into his farm clothes and sat down to smoke his pipe and get good-natured. He remarked, with a sigh, "Live and learn. No more city help for us, we must get someone who grew up in the back woods."

This was easier said than done and after several unsuccessful trials we decided that the fates demanded one more attempt at the city. I must tell you that the only reason we could afford help was the low wages at the time, three dollars a week for general housework, including washing. We could never have paid present day wages.

Poor Dad summoned all his good nature and his courage and set forth once more for New Haven. The girls called after him, "Don't get a fine lady this time. Get a homely old woman." He grinned and waved goodbye, and when he returned at evening he had with him a tall, gaunt, sober-faced Scotch woman by the name of Joanna. She looked as if she could cook a meal or scrub a floor and we plucked up courage.

Joanna proved very good and quiet and liked to stay out in the summer kitchen by herself and cook her meals out there on an old stove.

One Saturday I heard voices out there and wondered what company she was having. I investigated and found Joanna talking and laughing with a woman and three small children. She held a baby in her arms and told me proudly that her sister and the children had come out to enjoy the country. I was surprised, of course, but realized that they needed the country and also that we would have to share our dinner with them. I was quite sure our small steak would not go around, so I gave Joanna a slice of ham and some eggs and told her to cook vegetables and give them their dinner in the summer kitchen.

The children played all the afternoon in the orchard and stuffed themselves with the ripe pears that were lying on the ground. Jerry and the boys went out there and played with the youngsters and all had a good time. I was glad to let them enjoy our nice place but I wondered if Joanna would remember that the evening train left at seven o'clock. I went out to remind her and was smilingly told that they were going to stay all night and spend Sunday.

"But Joanna," I said, "Where can they all sleep?"

"Oh we'll sleep in my room if you'll let me have a mattress to lay on the floor."

I was somewhat overcome by this announcement and by having Joanna so able to do the honors, but I thought I might as well do my share of fresh air work, so I went up attic and brought out my old cradle for the baby and laid a mattress on the floor for the children. The two women would share the bed. It was hot up there but not so bad as in the city. They all slept peacefully and we heard no squalls of infants.

When I went down in the evening and told the family of our guests in the attic, the father said, "Of course it's all right. We must help the poor city people to have a little change." The girls sniffed scornfully and thought Joanna had cheek to import such a family.

Sunday morning the visitors were up early and the youngsters out eating pears again. I wondered how many they could eat without getting sick, but decided not to worry about them. The question of another dinner came to my mind, and as I knew our roast was too small I gave Joanna ham and eggs again and said they could drink plenty of milk. They kept out of our way and I saw to it that Joanna understood the visit was now over. They were called in at five o'clock and I helped wash their faces and pin up their torn clothes and they departed with large bag of pears and apples, happy to have had a country weekend, though those things had not yet become so popular.

"Well," I said, "We have now done our share of fresh air work." I suggested to Joanna, however, that the visit had better not be repeated, and she acknowledged that it was quite a task for her as well as me.

Joanna lasted quite a while and then she got some ailment which made her want to leave. We had other help on and off, but the girls had a chance to learn all about housework and that proved useful in after days.

Church Work (Black Hall)

In this pleasant place there was a temptation to just enjoy life through the summer. You might think from what I have written that the parson spent all his time farming and having a good time with his family, but of course his chief duty was to build up the Episcopal Church along the shoreline of Connecticut. When he took the position of missionary, there was no Episcopal service held between New London and Saybrook. Now he had work started in three places: Black Hall, South Lyme and Niantic. He also held occasional services in Noank for the ship builders and in Mystic, where there was an old parish. He found a place called Jerusalem because there were so many Jews living in it – but there were also Christians who wanted religious services. He never went to any place where other denominations were established, only to those where there were no Christian services.

There was no church of any kind in Black Hall, and that was the center of his work. He was home the first Sunday of every month for morning service and Communion, and went to South Lyme or Nyantic in the afternoon. That seemed a proper Sunday to me, the children could be turned loose in the afternoon to enjoy themselves and I could get a little rest.

On the other Sundays, Theo went to South Lyme or Niantic in the morning, or to one of the far away stations, and came back for Sunday School and evening prayer, beginning at four o'clock.

Sarah Bartlett played the piano for services when she could not find some good excuse for not doing so. Then she demanded that I do it. I did not mind playing when I was well enough and had been used to doing it in Putnam. But I did not like her backing out and calling me a "snide" when I wanted her to do it. The Black Hall school boys went to Lyme Congregational church in the mornings and came to evening prayer at the Guild Room, and helped with the singing. I had a class in Sunday School and the children had good teachers.

The Sundays that Theo went away in the morning were a trial to me. He had to start early and we had a long day and I missed going to church in the morning. We had not yet advanced to the idea of Sunday as a purely holiday occasion and I felt that I ought to make it a different day for the children, but of course they wanted to play around as on other days, not being obliged to be dressed up in the morning. I compromised by having a short period of Bible readings and other readings outdoors, sometimes up on Meeting House hill (the name at least being appropriate to Sunday). Here they could lie around in the sun by the brook while I read, and between times explore the caves. Sometimes we sat in the open door of the big barn where the sweet scent of new mown hay mingled with the salt breath from the sea.

I read poems or stories which I thought they ought to know and they colored pictures and were treated to nibbles of maple sugar, which Dad ordered every spring – one of our few treats. Jerry said afterwards that whenever she read the "Vision of Sir Launfal" it brought back to her those Sundays in the big barn and the scent of salt and hay. We had a late dinner and then it was hard to get the children clean and ready for Sunday School at four. They were tired and did not feel like being dressed up.

The Guild Room was used on weekdays for entertainments and the library was free to anyone who wanted books. One of the neighbor women started a sewing school and taught the little girls to make their own underclothes. Some of their work was sent also to a city mission. Our girls went as a matter of duty, but did not like to sew on flannel petticoats which always seemed to be in the works. Even our girls were not yet emancipated from underclothes.

Sometimes there was an evening sociable held in the rooms, when Theo tried to get the neighbors together and encouraged them to play games. Before we got through he had done this and had even taught them to dance the Virginia Reel to get them out of their rut. Some people, no doubt, thought it very wrong for a minister to teach dancing. He considered it a part of social service -- the neighbors down there had so little fun and enjoyment in their hard lives. You must remember this was before the days of movies, and no entertainments ever came there.

Once a year we had a rummage sale for the benefit of the mission, and we all thought it great fun. The well to do ladies from Lyme sent in their cast-off garments, perfectly good as a rule. There was a great rush on the part of the neighborhood ladies to get in first and have their pick. Once, I remember, we had a great time trimming over old hats and produced a fine show of millinery, which delighted the hearts of the women. We had to smile at the picture some of them made in their new finery, but it was great fun trimming the hats. One winter we even tried a women's exchange, where the good cooks brought samples of their best breads and cakes to be sold. Even I made a little money with entire wheat rolls, ginger drops and sponge cakes, when the ladies from Lyme came down to patronize the sale.

Old Lyme was an aristocratic neighbor a mile or more up the street, but I was never introduced there as we had no people living in that section. The Old Lyme church, Congregational, was and still is one of the most beautiful specimens of Colonial architecture, and the Congregational system so ruled the town that there was no room for Episcopalians. Mr. Bartlett's second wife being a member of that church rather diminished his active interest in our mission.

Theo tried to teach the people the Church Year, which was new to most of them. He could not keep the full list of special days, but always had service on Thanksgiving and Christmas and had a tree for the children on some day near Christmas. He started the observance of Ascension Day and All Saints. This was new to them all and the All Saints festival appealed to them at once. He taught them the meaning of remembering the dead on this day, and had them bring flowers for the altar which were afterward laid on the graves of their dear ones. They liked the custom and kept it up even after we had left.

Easter of course was a great day, and he tried to be home in the morning and make the other missions have afternoon services, which did not always please them, but he thought the family had some rights and he wanted to be with us in the morning.

South Lyme was a small settlement between Black Hall and Niantic, and there was no service there except what Theo could furnish. The Methodist Church was closed. The small congregation of Episcopalians and any others who would come met in the school house Sunday afternoon and had service without a choir, only a small melodeon to lead – when they could get anyone to play it.

When Bishop Brewster came to visit the missions, I went with him and Theodore to South Lyme and saw how primitive the conditions were. The Bishop and the missionary put on their vestments in the front entry, walked through the room and mounted the platform where there was just the teacher's desk and a chair. The parson raised the tune for the hymns and we stood up to sing, raising the seats behind us – the regular school chairs – and when we sat down they dropped with a bang. The Bishop preached just as well as if he were in a lovely chancel. There was no confirmation at that time, as they had not been taught long enough.

I have heard Theo tell about the first time he went to the school house to hold a service. He found the door locked and no one in sight. He and his companion got in through a window and found there was no fire. It was cold weather, so they chopped up the schoolhouse broom for kindling, brought some sticks from the wood pile and had the place warm before the people got there. The janitor had failed in his duty for some reason. Of course the parson replaced the broom afterwards and the people learned they had to get the place ready on time.

After a year or two the congregation got so large that they demanded a chapel. It was built by the missionary society, a small building in a grove of cedars. Theodore thought Cedar Grove Chapel would be a good name for it, but some of the ambitious ones wanted it called St. Cecilia's Chapel. Judging from the music I heard there the name seemed rather far-fetched, though they had a small cabinet organ and a choir of mixed voices. At least they did their best and no doubt the music was acceptable to Saint Cecilia.

These were small undertakings, but at least religion was being taught to people who had no other opportunity, and your father had the gift of speaking simply and interestingly and holding people's attention. I think some of them heard the principles of the Christian Life taught for the first time. You must remember that there were no automobiles at that time and that ordinary people had no horses, so could not drive miles to church. I think that mission has been abandoned, now that transportation has changed, and people can go to a church several miles away.

Niantic was another place the missionary had to work up. Professor MacCook of Trinity college had a summer home on the bay and for several years had been holding services in his house on Sunday. Now there was such a large group of people that a chapel was demanded. One was put up by the missionary society, Theo helping to raise the money, and it was then included in his list of missions. Like the Guild room, the chapel was a combination for church and weekday work, a library and room for social gatherings as well as a chancel.

Miss Alice Bush, an enterprising enthusiastic schoolteacher , was the leader of the effort. While she did great work, like some other devoted people she sometimes drove a little too hard. After Theo's day she made considerable trouble. I remember after we left there he had a letter from Bishop Brewster asking some questions about the mission and saying that Miss Bush was acting like the devil. Too bad that saints sometimes go so far as to become sinners.

One thing was a great satisfaction to Theodore, that in all these missions he succeeded in teaching them to give for general missionary work. In after years he was so pleased when he saw in the reports that his missions had kept up their good habits and always paid their share of the apportionment. In the winter we sometimes had a social gathering at the Manse, hoping to get better acquainted with the people. Some of the young masters at the school would venture to come and help with music and games. Nan played the piano for them to sing and the young men were induced to sing solos. I remember "Alice Ben Bolt" being sung by one of them, which was no doubt interesting to Alice. We had games and refreshments. The neighbors called the house the Lighthouse, because it stood on high ground and our lamplight shone out over the dark street and meadows. We wanted to make it a real lighthouse of hope and cheer, but I don't know how well we succeeded. It was hard to overcome the shyness and sensitivity of the country people, so easily offended.

Theo of course visited the sick, but I was not called upon often for that. I remember once he came and told me of a whole family down with measles and I must cook something for them and come with him to their house. I did not know what they would want but thought they ought to have some cereal and gelatin. I made some and went with the parson. To my amazement we were greeted by three or four children with rash on their faces. They were gathered around the kitchen table about to devour a large chocolate cake some neighbor had brought in. They were all coughing but the oldest sister said they were all right and getting well. I could not give any orders and did not mention the cereal etc., but I did get some off on the mother, who was in bed with a small baby, both broken out with measles. She seemed grateful for some invalid food and I cleaned up the baby and made the mother more comfortable. How they did need a visiting nurse!

Our Visitors

That first summer we had no visitors but the next summer all our relatives and friends wanted to see our home, especially as it was by the salt water and meant beach and swimming. I remember my brother Fred coming on one of his rare visits north, and I have pictures of Margaret and Theodore on the beach with our crowd.

The cousins, Esther and Jeanne, just the ages of Nan and Alice, came for a visit and they all had a grand time. The four slept in the big spare bedroom and carried on at a great rate. I remember Dad yelling at them to stop playing golf in their night gowns and threatening to come in and paddle them, which threat was greeted with snorts of mirth and much giggling.

One day they explored the attic and turned the trunks upside down for costumes, and after rigging themselves up in the most stylish and extravagant way, paraded around in the meadows, causing passers-by to gaze in astonishment.

Then one moonlight night they begged to sleep in the barn and we consented. They played great pranks, riding Jenny bare-back, much to her disgust, and dancing with bare feet in the moonlight. The younger members of the family were quite offended that the elders were allowed so much liberty while they had to go to bed in the house.

I remember how I had to cook during this visit. We had no maid at the time and I baked great sheets of gingerbread and cake as well as many loaves of bread. The girls were watching one day as I drew a large tin of fragrant gingerbread from the oven and Jeanne said, "You make the best gingerbread of anybody in the world," and Esther added, "and the best cake," so I knew that my labors were appreciated.

The girls begged to be allowed to drive Jenny to the beach by themselves, and though I was a good deal afraid of what

might happen, Dad decided to let them try it. His condition
was that one should ride backwards to watch out for automobiles and if one came, they must turn in to the nearest place
and let it go by. Lady Jane was so afraid of them that it would
be dangerous to be on the road with one. Fortunately they
were still very scarce and there was not much chance of
meeting one, so I watched them drive off in the two-seat
wagon, one sitting backwards, all wearing large white sun
bonnets with capes which had just become stylish. I was
uneasy until they returned, but nothing went wrong with the
excursion.

Dad now proposed that we have a sail and they all agreed
with enthusiasm. Fortunately for my peace of mind, he
engaged the captain of a sailboat to take us. I would not have
dared trust the family on the briny deep with their father as
skipper, though he would have been much offended if I had
said so. We drove to the Lyme wharf and got aboard with large
baskets of lunch. The breeze was fresh and we sailed out into
the Sound in fine style, ate our lunch and enjoyed the motion
of the waves. The boys had to explore everything, of course,
and the captain was good to them and let them climb around
while he kept an eye on them. The sun got very hot at noon and
the breeze died down and then we found sailing was not so
pleasant. The sails flapped idly in the feeble breeze and the
boat rocked to and fro, causing very queer feelings in some of
the stomachs. The sun beat down on our heads and the small
boys began to fret and one of the girls was sick. We all felt
decidedly queer but tried to keep up our spirits by singing
songs and whistling for a breeze, as we were told sailors did,
but it took a long time for the breeze to answer our invitation.
Dad told funny stories and we managed to endure life until the
evening breeze sprang up, the sails were filled, and we came
sailing home in great feather, having learned that there are
drawbacks, even to a life on the ocean waves. It was a change

anyway and we soon forgot the discomforts.

Dad was always taking the girls out in the rowboat and sometimes they got caught at low tide on the muddy flats. One day when he was trying to push off with an oar he lost his balance and plunged in head foremost to their great alarm. He soon came up, sputtering and covered with mud, his straw hat floating behind him.

There was a foot bridge over the creek at one end and the favorite sport of small boys was to cross it, knowing that they might fall off but yearning to show their skill at keeping on. One day Jerry was with them and all three decided to try it. Billy was carrying his battered old baseball and bat and Jerry told him he would have to leave it behind but he refused to part with it and they started across. Billy was behind the others and soon there was a splash and in he went, bat and all, and had to be rescued and brought home. He had on new corduroy trousers and they were like a wet cat. He had to go to bed while they were dried as he had no other play suit.

There was one peculiar little visitor who came about once a year – Theo's cousin Mary Ruth Close of Brooklyn, a real character of the Hetty Green type. She had inherited quite a fortune from her father, Uncle George Close, who made his money by inventing patent medicines. She lived in an old house near the Navy Yard, the windows and blinds kept closed, not a ray of light coming in, and being half blind, she kept lamps lighted all day. Her only companion was a girl as queer as herself who had a bad temper and sometimes they flew at each other like two mad hens and pulled each other's hair. She was very penurious, spending hardly any money and living in the poorest way, eating with steel knives and forks because she hoarded the family silver in a safe place, indulging in no luxuries of any kind.

Mary wore her great grandmother's clothes, also her grandmother's and her mother's, and never bought anything new, just rummaged in her trunk for clothes. She was generous, however, to other people, gave large sums for the home for the blind and other charities and she sent Dad ten dollars every month to keep up his insurance policy, a wonderful help with money so scarce. When she came to see us the children had to run away once in a while to control their risibilities, she was so quaint and funny in her old fashioned clothes, her hair combed smoothly back and rolled in a knob at the back, looking like a little old woman, though no older than I, about forty. She would tell in detail how many petticoats she had on and sometimes would sit down in the road and pull up her dress to count them, to the great embarrassment of Nan and Alice if they were with her. She wore blue glasses and a funny little bonnet and carried a small black satchel with an assortment of medicine bottles which she would take out and describe and recommend to us. They were mostly laxatives which her father had patented.

It was rather a strain on the family to keep from laughing while she was there and after she left there would be a burst of merriment, but we did appreciate Mary Ruth's good qualities. She was loyal to the Peck family and when she died some years later, she left Dad the legacy which he had been saying jokingly for many years that he expected. He did not really expect a legacy, but said it to encourage us when times were hard, and when it came, only he and I were left at home to enjoy it but it was a wonderful relief in our old age to be independent of charity and to be able to help our children in their efforts to get started in life. We spent rather freely for a while and enjoyed some of the vacations we had never been able to take, going to our beloved Inn In the Pines each winter for a few weeks. If Dad had not lost his sight we really would have travelled, but it was too hard for him as he could not see. Mary Ruth saved her money to good purpose for it helped Theodore and me and Aunt Clara to have relief from poverty in our old age. All honor to the queer little woman.

Another visitor was Aunt Clara and she was always welcome, the children being so fond of her and she so ready to enter into all their doings. She still remembers the parties under the apple trees in the orchard, Alice's May birthdays with outdoor supper and a big angel cake, because the hens were laying well just then. She was working for her living at that time but sometimes got away to visit us.

Our Christmas guests were Harold Deane and Auntie Mary, who took Harold as her boy after his mother's death. She liked to bring him to our house at Christmas because she knew he would have a good time. She was a dearly beloved Aunt and so full of fun and jollity she was always a welcome guest. The children looked forward to this visit with great joy and joined in all the preparations for the holidays, Dad taking the younger ones out to the woods to get pine and laurel and cut a Christmas tree. He always sawed a big log to be brought in on Christmas Eve as a yule log.

Mother was stirring the big fruit cake with the girls' help. Raisins had to be seeded in those days and currants cleaned, citron sliced. Mincemeat was made from our own apples, and negotiations were under way for a turkey from some farmer.

I had to take the boys and Marjorie shopping in New London and that was quite a feat. Each one had a small sum of money in a purse and I must know just what they spent and if they got the right change and see that no one on the list was forgotten, and that no child knew what was bought for him or her – quite a job for a mother. In the crowded stores and with all the excitement it was hard to keep accounts straight and see that no packages were lost. I tried to do my own shopping at another time as it was quite enough to look after the youngsters.

Going on the train was a treat to them also. Reaching home

tired but triumphant, there was a great looking over of packages, counting of lists and wrapping of presents.

The boys were curled up on the floor by the fire that evening and I heard Ted say to Billy, "Say, Bill, don't you wish you knew what I bought for you?"

"What?" said Billy.

"I'll tell you this much, it's something drawing something, but I won't tell you what."

"Oh, say, how funny, that's the same thing I got for you, something drawing something, but I won't tell you what." Christmas morning revealed that the "something" was an iron dog drawing an iron monkey and an iron monkey drawing an iron dog. They managed to keep from telling the whole thing and were duly surprised at stocking time.

The day before Christmas the house was decorated with wreaths of ground pine and bunches of laurel, the table spread with the best cloth for the traditional Christmas Even supper, the big fruit cake in the center with a bunch of laurel in the middle, and candles on each side ready to be lighted. Aunt Mary and Harold came in out of the cold, Harold's cheeks red and shining, his overcoat buttoned up to his chin, his eyes dancing, Aunt Mary smiling broadly, as jolly as ever. We had a merry supper, then the stockings were hung by the fireplace and the traditional "Night before Christmas" read and then the youngsters were packed off to bed and I worked late, doing last things and making decorations for the tree. Mary thought I did too much when she saw me making cornucopias for the candies – even those were homemade.

Early in the morning the laughing crew, shouting "Merry Christmas," got their elders up and came down in procession to open the bulging stockings. No matter how tired and sleepy Dad and Mother were, they always got up and led the procession.

I remember Aunt Mary expressing surprise and admiration

at the pleasure the boys and girls got out of such small and inexpensive gifts. Alice was in raptures over a roll of music that cost one dollar, Nan beaming over a new paint box, Jerry hugging new books and the boys shouting over a long tin train, not electric. Aunts and grandparents had sent small gifts and all were as happy as if millions of dollars had been spent.

We all went to church in the Guild Room and sang the Christmas hymns and carols, then hastened home to see if the turkey was still in the oven. According to the boys it might have been carried off by a hungry tramp, but we found it there all right, and oh, what a whiff of appetizing odor when the oven door was opened. The young ones went sliding while we prepared the dinner, and then Papa carried in the turkey with the family following in procession, sniffing with rapture. After the blessing they must wait with patience for the carving to be done and we liked to quote the young Cratchitts at Tiny Tim's Christmas dinner, "stuffing spoons into their mouths to keep from screaming for stuffing." Drumsticks went to the boys, as usual, and soon all were helped. We gave ourselves up to feasting and merriment, then at dusk went to the big parlor where the tree was waiting, lighted with real candles and hung with homemade ornaments and candy bags. More presents, as I had reserved some for this time, and exclamations of joy. We always had to sing "Gather Around the Christmas Tree," as that had been the old custom in the family. The toys and games were spread out around the tree and played with all the evening while the elders, having paused to wash the dishes, relaxed and indulged in new books and candy.

Harold enjoyed these visits, all the sports and jollity, and said he would rather spend Christmas at the Pecks' than anywhere else – there was "always something doing at the Pecks.'" We did not have to rush around in autos or run to the movies – there were no movies and no autos, so we had to amuse ourselves at home.

You will recognize that some of these customs, at least, are being preserved in one daughter's home, the Rooftree having inherited the traditions and being a gathering place for as many of the family as can get there. We are scattered pretty widely now, but still cherish the memory of the old Christmases.

Schools

All through that first pleasant summer the question of schools had been in our minds, and as September approached we had to decide what we were to do about our children's education. Send them to boarding school we could not and there were no very good schools in our town. A Miss Griswold kept a girl's boarding school in Lyme but no day scholars were admitted. The boys were too young for Bartlett School and the district school in Black Hall was of the most primitive type. There was a good public school in Lyme and we decided that the older girls would have to go there for a year anyway. I did so long to have them get the good education which I got at St. Margaret's, but that would have to wait.

We got a bicycle for the girls to ride, taking turns, and in bad weather Dad would have to transport them. The next year we could have a scholarship from the Woman's Auxiliary of one hundred dollars from the fund to assist clergymen's daughters, and that would enable Nan to go to the Williams Institute in New London, a free academy for girls. The one hundred would pay her car fare and her board through the week, and she could come out on the train Friday night. The girls had to take their luncheons and stay all day. I had a great time trying to make them take a bottle of milk, but they refused because no girls were so babyish!

As to the younger children, Marjorie was still too nervous to be shut up in school more than half day, and Ted was rather delicate after his long illness in Putnam and needed much fresh air. Dad visited the school and could hardly bear the thought of their going to such a place. He said he would not be willing to keep his cow in such a dilapidated building, and the teacher was not trained and the children so disruptive that he hated to have our children with them. However, we decided that the law would require us to send them somewhere, as we had not time to teach them at home. Billy was too young to go, but Ted and Marjorie would have to go half a day.

After the first term we were quite disgusted with the school, and when the superintendent sent us a complaint that our children were only half-day pupils, Theo got indignant and wrote the gentleman what he thought of the school, meeting in a building which he would be unwilling to keep his cow in, an incompetent teacher and a set of children he was not willing to have his own play with. He explained that the children had been ill and were not supposed to be shut up long. The official happened to be a doctor and he said he was glad to accept the excuses, for he knew things were not as they should be. It was most irritating to me that our children could not have good advantages, but we tried to make up for it by furnishing them good books at home and trying to stimulate their minds.

Food and Clothing

Clothing the family was quite a problem, for it took most of our money to buy the food and meet other expenses, and clothes would wear out, especially shoes, so the youngsters sometimes looked pretty shabby. We determined that they should be well fed whatever they had to go without and we worked out a scheme of mail orders for meat and groceries, paying less than was demanded in the local stores. There was no market in Black Hall, only a cart which came through from Lyme every other day, and the prices were high. Theo had learned at Pomfret School about a wholesale meat firm in New York and we could have big roasts of beef and chunks of corned beef or legs of lamb, etc, sent out once or twice a week. We also got coffee unground in ten pound bags from Garretson and so saved quite a bit. We had our own milk, eggs and fruit which was a great help. Our meals were plain but wholesome and the children grew rosy and plump.

Clothes were a different matter. There never seemed to be any money left for those and I had to plan carefully, patch and darn and make over, get out a pair of small trousers from a serge skirt, cut down the big girls' things for Jerry, and almost never have anything new myself.

Now the Church came to the rescue, as in the school dilemma. Bishop Brewster had established a pet charity in the diocese of Connecticut, called the Comfort Club, and I can testify that it was well-named. Its sole object was comfort for the clergymen's families living on small salaries, especially those with numerous children. Miss Sarah Davies of Hartford was the head of this Club and I wish for my own satisfaction to record what a blessing she was to us. It was provided that she alone knew what families were being benefited, and there could be no embarrassment between givers and receivers.

She got from the Bishop a list of clergy who he thought needed this help. She then wrote to the mother of the family and asked for a list of the children by name and age, and then she sent a blank to be filled out with a list of articles needed for each and their sizes. Also there was a blank for myself and my household needs and even measurement blanks for the clergyman himself, which he was to send to a special clerical tailor in New York if he needed a suit made. I don't know how else the parson would have been properly clothed.

In due course of time a box arrived, and what a gala day that was! The family gathered around with thrills of expectancy while the parson wielded the hammer until the lid was off. They fell upon the contents, each snatching what she or he thought was theirs, while I stood by and laughed and let them rummage, but eventually took hold myself and fitted clothes to proper owners. There were often entirely new things, especially underwear and stockings, and even dresses. Some of the clothes were second hand but always good and acceptable. Sometimes, however, the girls were not pleased because a dress or coat was out of fashion. They had an antipathy to jackets with protruding tails behind, which had been in style but were now out of date. They called them "jay-birds" and refused to wear them. There were secondhand dresses of fine material which could be made over and were often just the thing for parties and visits. The girls were clever at making over and in this way got costumes which we could never have afforded to buy.

Sometimes there would be a new outfit for me, dress and coat and all, which was wonderful, as I went months without buying anything new. I remember one box which had a new outfit for Jerry and the boys – a pretty sailor suit for her and suits for the boys as well as plenty of stockings. After sitting up nights to patch pants and darn stockings, sometimes even having to darn a hole on the leg Sunday morning, it was such a relief to spread out those new garments and know that they would be well dressed for Sunday. I think the Comfort Club is not as active now that the salaries of married men have been raised, and even in the mission field it is thought best to send money and not clothes, but in my own case it saved me the worry of going away to shop and also it stimulated our clever-ness in making over things, so I do not feel any shame in telling about it.

Alice's husband in later years expressed himself strongly on the subject of making minister's families objects of charity. It offended him to think that his wife in her girlhood had been subjected to that kind of help. I said to him, "You are a

Vestryman, are you not?" He said "yes," and I remarked, "Then see to it that the clergy are paid enough so that charity won't be necessary." That Comfort Club certainly lightened my burdens as a missionary's wife and it has been a pleasure to me since then to pack missionary boxes, knowing what goes on at the other end.

Our money for magazines and books was very scarce. We had a fairly good library and some aunties always gave books at Christmas, but we could not indulge in new books very often and I had to guard the parson from book agents and magazine vendors. He found it hard to resist them and when a man came getting subscriptions for a large work called "The Animate Creation," to be delivered in monthly sections and then bound, he was greatly tempted, and thought it would be a very valuable thing for the children to have. I stood behind the agent, making faces and threatening gestures to warn Theo, but it was no use, he fell for it and we were loaded up with monthly payments for a year. The worst of it was that the children did not care for it. They would look at it once and then put it away, and they complained that it told about strange animals all over the world but did not tell about the birds and creatures they wanted to know about. The words "Animate Creation" became anathema in the family. One Sunday Dad, by some subconscious twist of mind, spoke the words "Animate Creation" in his sermon on the wonders of God's world, and the family mutually shuddered and looked out of the corners of their eyes at each other, suppressing their grins. We moved that bunch of literature around till we could not bear the sight of it and then cast it out, to the Salvation Army or some such place, I have forgotten. That experience cured Dad of listening to book agents for a while anyway.

The Law

I must now record a tragic incident in our lives, the loss of our beloved wagon, the two-seater and excursion wagon and also our first contact with the law. Dad had engaged some men to do some work for him around the barn and had made a bargain with them for so much pay, but they had no written contract, and when they demanded their pay they were not satisfied with what was handed out and claimed that the work was worth more than that. Dad stuck to the price which had been agreed upon and refused to raise it. They threatened to "have the law on him," and got his back up and he refused to pay more. They went away breathing out threats, and one day soon after that a great burly man stepped up as Dad was out by the barn and, pointing to a badge on his coat, said "I'm the consta-bull." It was our neighbor, Mr. Bump, who with an air of great authority announced that Mr. Peck would have to stand trial for unpaid wages, breach of promise, etc., and if the case went against him the wagon would be seized in payment. He proceeded to put a tag on the wagon and turned away. My brother Fred happened to be there and was an interested spectator. He saw Theo's face getting pretty red and whispered to him, "Shall I punch him? Shall I punch him?" but Dad thought it better not to get rough.

He went to New London and put the case in the hands of his lawyer friend, Will Stark, told him his side of it and thought of course he would bring it out all right. Will Stark was a good friend of the family and often ran out on the train to have supper with us. He liked our fried mush and molasses and big baked apples. I don't know why he failed in this case but after several trials the case was decided in favor of the plaintiffs and the poor parson had to accept defeat.

It was a bitter pill for him and the family. We were all very mad and aired our opinions of the law with great vigor. It was a sad day when we had to endure the humiliation of seeing our beloved wagon sold at auction by the side of the road. We were huddled in a bunch on the hillside just above the road and looked on with inward maledictions as the bidding rose. The reaction of the family was, "the law is no good."

Health

We got through the first winter without illness except croupy colds on the children's part, but in February of the next winter the grippe seized me and I had a long illness, with the worst cough I ever had. I was racked day and night with it and in my tired condition my nerves gave out and I was quite prostrated. The young doctor at Lyme tried everything he could think of and after a few weeks hit on a medicine which did help and I got better, but was too weak to get up.

Alice had to stay out of school and do the house work with a woman coming in sometimes. Nan was in New London all the week. Dad was keeping well but very busy, having to go to Church meetings and be away a good deal. One day he was summoned for the laying of a corner stone somewhere. It was March, cold and stormy, and it rained the day he went. I felt worried all day and when he got home at night he came right upstairs and I was horrified at his looks. I knew he was sick. He said he did not want any supper, undressed and got into bed with me and went off into a heavy sleep. He had been sleeping on the other side of my bed as he had to wait on me at night and there was no room for a cot, and no adjoining room. It was most unsanitary and I can imagine the horror of "you-all" when I mention it.

He snored all night, so hoarsely that I feared diphtheria, especially as he said his throat was sore. When I touched him he was burning hot. I lay awake all night wondering what I ought to do. He was still muttering and tossing in the morning and did not wake up. Alice brought my breakfast and was able to make him take a little coffee.

Dr. Burnham was coming to see me, so we did not send for him and when I heard him running up the stairs I wondered what he would say. He stopped short and stared a minute, began to laugh, but put his hand over his mouth, then said, "Do my eyes deceive me or are there two in that bed?" "Yes, doctor," I said, "and I don't know what to do about it."

He proceeded to examine Theodore and then said, "Well, as you both have the same thing, you may as well stay together as I don't see any other way. You ought to have a nurse but I don't know where to find one."

I said I thought we would have to stay together so that I could look after <u>him</u>, and the doctor agreed and proceeded to lay out medicines for me on one side of my table and some for Theo on the other side, putting placards on them so I would not get mixed up. Then he called Alice and delivered his orders to her. "Don't let your Mother get up, don't let your Father get up, and try to make something nice for them to eat."

This was a hard order for a thirteen year old girl who was already doing the house work, but she agreed to do her best. Theo slept most of the day, and I lay and wondered what I ought to do. It seemed rather a desperate situation and I decided to write home and see if they could suggest anything. Alice brought me a pad and pencil and I wrote Mother of our sad plight and asked her advice.

Meanwhile, I called Jerry and told her that she and the boys must go and find Mr. Bump or Mr. Bramble and ask them to take care of the horse and cow and bring the milk. Then they must feed the hens and bring in the eggs themselves. After a while they came in and stood by the bed with such solemn faces that I wondered what was the matter. Jerry spoke up: "The hens won't stop laying long enough for us to get the eggs."

That struck me as so funny I began to laugh and, being

weak, kept on laughing, which waked up Theo and he began to laugh and we shook the bed with our hysterics, to the great astonishment of the children.

In the morning a telegram came from Father: "Nurse coming on evening train." This was joyful news to me but the youngsters looked rather doubtful. Billy remarked, "I don't like nurses." Jerry ventured to ask, "Will she be cross?"

I had a sudden vision of a starched, particular, trained nurse in our disordered house, but I was pretty sure Father would not have sent that kind. I calmed their fears with a picture of a nice lady who would get them some good meals and make us all more comfortable.

Next I consulted with Alice as to where the nurse could sleep, and told her that I could not bear to have a strange nurse come and find Dad and me in the same bed. I thought we must get a fire made in the big guest room and move me in there. We could put up a cot in there for the nurse. I knew it would be a good change for me to get out of that fever-heated bed and into a fresh one. Alice agreed and set about making a fire in the little coal stove. This was new work for her and proved very trying. The fire went out and she made it over again, and as soon as she left it, out it went. She was chilled through and almost in tears when Mrs. De Wolf, our neighbor, came in to see if she could do anything for us, and I asked her to please help the poor child make a fire. She was used to the funny cylinder stoves and soon had a good fire. I asked her to help Alice make the bed and leave it open to get warm, which would take several hours as the room was so frigid. She said she would come again at five o'clock and help me.

Alice got dinner and when Mrs. De Wolf came back they put me into a rocking chair and drew me into the other room. As I was getting off, Dad waked up and protested in a sickly voice at my leaving him. "Oh, don't go, I want you here, I don't want to be alone," but I told him it wasn't good for me to be in his bed and there would be a nurse to take care of both of us, but he was like a child, whimpering for his Mama.

The big bed felt so chill in spite of the fire that I almost shivered but wrapped myself in a blanket. The medicines were now moved in and Alice consoled her father while Mrs. De Wolf tidied up his room. We all had supper and then listened for the train whistle. I had asked one of the neighbors to meet the train with our buggy, and when we heard the wheels the three youngsters hid behind various doors where they could peep out and not be seen, while Alice opened the door and admitted a smiling, rosy-faced, gray-haired English woman who hastened in, so glad to get out of the cold. She called Alice "My Dear" and asked where the children were. They ventured to come out from their hiding places and shake hands and then came running up to me in great excitement. "She's just a nice Grandma," they said and put away their fears.

She came up and looked over the situation and then went down and Alice made her a cup of tea and got her something to eat, which seemed to make a great impression on her. She spoke feelingly of that dear little girl doing everything and looking out for her so well. Alice and she became the best of friends and the whole family felt the uplift in having such a wholesome cheerful person in the house. Mrs. Hudson, or Auntie Hudson as we came to call her, was one of those comfortable persons who seem made to take care of the sick and cheer up the discouraged. We all felt better under her ministrations and Dad became much attached to her and stopped mourning over my desertion. She was much amused at the ways of our country neighborhood, having been in the city a long time. She couldn't get over laughing at the funny names of our neighbors, the Bumps and the Brambles, who were taking care of the horse and cow, and she thought the chickens very amusing. She would go out to look at them and would tell the children "the 'ens are cacklin' in their 'ouses," to their great amusement – they loved to hear her English way of speaking. She talked about her daughter "Halice" and spoke of our Alice the same way.

Auntie Hudson, bless her heart, got us out of our doldrums and when she left, Dad was able to be up and begin taking some of his duties, I was well enough to go downstairs and do a little, but I did not get strong and was still under the doctor's care in April. The grippe had settled on my weak nerves and kept me down. Dr. Burnham brought an older doctor from Saybrook to see me and they decided that I must go away from home and have hospital care. My father wanted to send me to the Clifton Springs Sanitarium in N.Y. state, but I could not bear to go so far from home and said I would rather go the Putnam Hospital and be under Dr. Morrell's care as he already knew me. That was arranged and Father said he should pay the bills.

Theo went up with me and saw some of his old friends in Putnam, and I settled down to hospital life, glad to feel that I could have the benefit of the institution my husband helped to found.

Dr. Morrell found that I needed some operative treatment, so I went through that and then just relaxed and enjoyed being nursed. Some of my old friends in Putnam came to see me and altogether I had a pleasant time.

At home things were not very easy, though Aunt Clara came to take charge and did the cooking. But Alice had to help and still stay out of school, though having an hour or two in the afternoon with Miss Nettie Bartlett, who kindly offered to give her English and History lessons. Alice was appointed to take care of the boys, and mend their stockings, darn their torn trousers and see that they were clean for meals, besides making beds, etc. She felt her responsibilities too much and when I got home I found her quite tired out and blue, so I consulted our doctor and he said to send her off for a visit.

Jean wanted her to come to New Haven, so she went there with her bicycle and had a good time riding and forgetting her cares.

Aunt Clara kept the family well fed and treated them to their favorite dishes. Ted wrote me while I was away such a funny letter and described all the goodies which he saw on the pantry shelf, lemon and cocoanut pies and layer cakes. He ended "My stomach sang softly to itself."

I recovered enough to take up my duties at home and in church and we went along all right through the summer, but the next winter was hard. The weather was very cold and rough, the wind blowing in such gales as I had never heard, that screech and whistle which the seashore wind indulges in, keeping shutters banging all night and really rocking the house at times. I could lie awake and imagine the ships out there in the dark being battered by the gale and found it hard to sleep. I was tired all the time and Theo was getting rheumatic with the long drives and exposure to sea winds, and he had frequent colds, almost bronchitis. He had resigned his position as Archdeacon, so the work was easier, but still he felt that he had done it long enough, and I was quite sure of it for my part. I longed to be in a parish again, in a city if possible, where the children could have good schools and more social advantages. I did not want them to be wild little country bumpkins and the girls needed more society. The only chance they had to go out was when the Bartlett School gave a winter dance and Miss Bartlett invited them. She knew they needed to be introduced to some kind of society and that they had not suitable clothes. She personally made a muslin dress for Nan, and a Comfort Club box came just then which contained a white India muslin dress for Alice with black velvet bows and she was delighted to wear it. They did not know how to dance or behave but made a valiant try at it, and Alice had a wonderful time. Nan was still stiff from her spinal trouble so could not

dance very well and felt rather shy and unhappy. Dad and I
went over to watch and bring them home. This broke the ice
but there was only one dance a year, so they really did need
more social advantages as well as higher education.

Moving Again

When Bishop Brewster made his fatherly visit, Theo put
the case before him and asked if he might resign his position as
missionary after twelve years. He told the bishop that he was
finding the work very hard, the exposure to sea winds and cold
were giving him rheumatism and his energies were flagging.
His family needed a different life and we would like to get back
to parish work if possible. Bishop did not like it much and said
he could not spare him as a missionary. Couldn't he put on the
steam and keep it up? Then I put in my plea and said I was
having too much illness and that the children were growing up
and needed more advantages. He began to consider it then, but
said it would be hard to get back into line for a parish after
being in other work so long. He would be on the lookout and
let us know.

This cheered us up to finish the winter but toward spring
another hard thing came along. Laurence and Marion, who
appeared as bride and groom in the Putnam chapter of this
history, had been through many hard experiences. They stayed
only one year in Putnam and did not make a success of it,
leaving the mission in poor shape. Laurence then went to
Philadelphia for a while, then to Massachusetts, where he got
out with Bishop Lawrence, as he did with nearly every bishop
he served under. Bishop Brewster refused to get him a parish
in Connecticut so he went west to Arkansas, to a mission field,
and there they had a hard time. A baby boy was born and after
nine months became very ill. Clara went out to help them, the
baby died, Laurence broke down, Marion was nearly ill and

they pulled up and came back east. They had no place to go, there was no other home in the family but ours, so of course they asked to come to us. I was feeling so tired and run down that I hesitated, but of course it was the only thing to do, so we gave them the invitation. They arrived, bag and baggage, and I gave them the big room upstairs. Laurence was so broken down that he had to have breakfast in bed, and Marion also slept late, then came down and carried up a tray to Laurence. She said the doctor had ordered extra nourishment for both of them and my heart sank, for it was already hard to keep enough to eat in the house. I remember saying to Theo one Monday morning that I had fourteen pounds of meat in the house Sunday and there was hardly enough to last over Monday.

Of course I was very sorry for them and did not begrudge the help we must give, but being so tired it wore on me to have to worry and also to hear the long, sad tales of their troubles, which Marion poured out. I began to feel very nervous and my heart symptoms returned, which worried me. I kept up my church work, but it was hard to drag around.

One day Miss Sally Lane, our good friend and benefactor, one of the best workers in the mission, came to see me, and got me in a corner alone, where she told me that she and her mother were worried about me and that her mother was going to give me fifty dollars and I must go away and stay till it was all spent. They were sure I was going to break down and have nervous prostration again if I did not get some rest. I demurred, of course, and said I could not leave these guests to take care of themselves, but she spoke very snappily about that and said they ought to be able now to take care of themselves, and with three girls in the house there was no reason why I could not leave. She had to argue with me quite a while and finally Theo was called in and he aided and abetted her, so I had to give in and say I would go somewhere. I wanted to go home to my father and mother, in their quiet home in Waterbury, so there I went and let them fuss over me, give me breakfast in bed, and I just relaxed and really rested.

Father and Mother wanted to go to Ocean Grove for a week or two, as Father enjoyed the meetings and music in the great tabernacle and also the indoor salt baths, and he thought those would be good for me, so I consented to go with them but in my tired condition it was too much of an effort and my heart behaved so badly while we were there that I was quite worried and had to keep very quiet. I was glad to get back to Waterbury and the little house. Then as my money was not used up, I felt like going to Marbledale and renewing in memory the old, romantic times there so I got Mrs. Tomlinson to take me in and had a good time reminiscing. I went home by way of Putnam and consulted Dr. Morrell. He said my heart was a nervous heart and there was no organic trouble, so I felt cheered up, and after visiting old friends there, I started for home. I knew the girls must have had a hard time and needed a holiday, so I sent word for them to meet me in New London and go out to Watch Hill for the day. Theo came with them and we had a nice day on the ocean beach. The girls told me all about their housekeeping under Aunt Marion's direction, which they did not enjoy. She did part of the cooking and taught them to do it also. She invited some of her grand New London friends out for the day and got up a big dinner. The girls baked a fish and made sauce for it under her directions, and the visitors were loud in their praises, so Nan and Alice thought they had learned something, but were very glad to get mother back and drop some of their cares. I was glad to hear that the Shermers had decided to move on, being much better in health, and Laurence would try to get a parish near Philadelphia.

I felt almost ashamed to have taken such a vacation and left the girls to work so hard, but my health had really improved so concluded it was a wise thing to do.

Nan had sprained her knee at tennis in New London and was on crutches the last part of the summer. She had made a good start in painting and did a good deal in oils, sitting with her foot up in a chair. She painted a panel of Theodore's handsome red and yellow corn, which we thought quite remarkable for a beginner.

We were clearing out rubbish and getting ready to pack up, hoping for some place to go, when Bishop Brewster wrote that he thought he had a place for Theo in New Haven. A small church which had been connected with a larger parish wanted to separate and have a minister of its own, so there was great rejoicing in the Peck family and we went right into the business of packing up to move. We were to go the first of August and then suddenly the Bishop wrote that the plan had fallen through and there was not a chance of being in New Haven. This was very sad, but we kept on packing up, trusting that some place would be offered. When people asked where we were going it was embarrassing to have to say we did not know. Our friends tried to dissuade us from going. Miss Lane pleaded that we could be just as well off in Black Hall and the children would soon be old enough to go the private schools, but she could not shake our desire to move.

For the first time in our lives we were all at sea, all packed up with nowhere to go. The family felt very sad and predicted that we would have to stay in the country after all. The girls groaned, "We'll always be country bumpkins and have no chance for school or society." The boys still stuck to their country loves – cows, cream, and the privilege of going barefoot, but the sisters scorned their remarks.

These doleful prophesies came true, for after a while the Bishop wrote rather apologetically that he had a place which very much needed such work as Mr. Peck knew so well how to do. There were two old parishes, Oxford and Quaker Farms, five miles apart, both run down and in bad condition, a great worry to him. If Mr. Peck would take hold there for a few years and put these places on their feet, then he felt sure he could get a better place for us. The Parson heaved a sigh at the prospect of the same kind of work he had been doing, and the family voiced its disappointment in loud and indignant remarks. As for me, my heart sank to my boots, for I had a mental picture of what it would mean, away back in the country, no companionship, no good schools. It was the first time in our history that I really hated to go to a new place. However, we made up our minds that it had to be, and braced ourselves for the change.

Much as I loved Bishop Brewster, I was really annoyed at his remark that our family could be just as healthy and happy in the country as in the city. As if he didn't know, I sputtered, that we had been living in the country all these years and needed a change. I imagine he did know it and was sorry for us but his own needs for the church work came first, of course.

It was Labor Day when the family moved and a bad day to be on the road. The trains were all late and we had to swelter in New Haven while waiting. Nan on crutches and her lame knee painful if bent, and all of us very hot and disgruntled. We were glad to get to Waterbury in the evening and rest our weary bones at Grandpa's house.

We could not move to Oxford directly as there was no rectory there or in Quaker Farms, and a suitable house could not be found right away. My father was determined that I should have an interval of easy life before going over there, so he rented for us a flat in a three family house near by where we could spend the winter, and he would put in the coal for us. Theo would go back and forth to Oxford on the train and keep the horse over there, so he could do his visiting, spend Sunday there and come back between times. Of course we had the best of it, it was not nice for him, but as usual he accepted it cheerfully.

Oxford and Quaker Farms
1902-1905

Interlude

This interlude planned for us so carefully by my dear
father, which in a way was a good change for me, was rather
disappointing. For one thing my family was for the first time
separated, the father boarding in Oxford half the week, and the
children and I in the apartment on Willow Street. For the first
time the family lived in a flat, second story with a long flight of
stairs. Nan being on crutches stayed with grandma for a while.
The children had at last a chance for a good school nearby.
Alice could use her scholarship of $100 for St Margaret's
school. My sister Mary had planned great things for me
socially, going to Women's Club of which she was president –
meeting fine people and getting out of my backwoods rut.

The first great event was the Golden Wedding of my
mother and father, a great occasion planned and carried out
mainly by Mary, the genius of the family. She got up a golden
book consisting of writing and poems by the Abbott brothers,
nieces and nephews. My contribution, on her orders, was a
poetical dedication and the story of my childhood in the old
first home. Nieces wrote poems, Nan and Alice were dis-
patched to Watertown to the old Merriman house to make
sketches, and Mary even broke into poetry and got a musician
to set it to music. Fine photos were taken from old time
daguerreotypes and Mary passed no end of time and money on
the project. The book was bound in white leather and Nan
decorated the cover, her first attempt at illustration. She and

Alice made pen and ink sketches of Nancy's early life in
Watertown. It was a wonderful production and is much
admired in the family. I am its keeper at present.

The great day came and absent sons and daughters came
home. Fred brought his tow-headed daughters Josephine and
Charlotte. Uncle Ben and Aunt Lil came from California. We
took some of the boys into our house, Kate was living nearby
and could harbor some of the guests. We had a family dinner,
after all going to church together. There were speeches by the
Abbott brothers, poems read, the Golden Book presented and a
white and gold set of china, hand painted and bearing the
monogram of the happy couple on each piece.

The next day there was a picnic in the yard at which time
all relatives within reach were welcomed. Nan got around on
crutches and entertained. In the evening there was a reception
for neighbors and friends.

The boys all piled in and out coming in from time to time
for another dish of ice cream. I saw many old friends and must
say I was delighted but I was so tired I could hardly get up the
hill to go home. I was having trouble with the change of life,
and had to give up often and lie on the bed.

I must describe the apartment. It had a good-sized living
room with a big window looking out on the street, a large
dining room that served as work and playroom, and a good
kitchen with washtubs set in, water supply and electric lights,
all of which were a joy after our primitive house in Black Hall.
It had three bedrooms, side by side, quite small. Dad and I had
one, the three girls another and the two boys in the last room.
As usual Jerry was the odd number and had to be squeezed in
with her sisters on a cot. Dressing was hard in these close
quarters, but we got along.

The children started school and all went well until Billy
began to whoop. Whooping cough had broken out in school.
Ted was quarantined, and eventually Marjorie too. They all

whooped it up together. Alice was sent to Grandma but soon began to cough and so lost a term of her precious St. Margaret's. She kept up her studies at home and I tried to help the whooping children with their lessons. It was funny at meals when someone told a joke and the whole bunch got to laughing and ran away from the table whooping and shouting. This lasted until Christmas. Then we had a good dinner with Grandma and Grandpa and Uncle John. I was able to get downtown shopping to my great joy. I remember how good it was to see the windows and decorations after my long sojourn in country towns.

After the holiday the children went back to school. Alice was happy again at St. Margaret's. Then came another blow. Jerry came home with a sore throat and I saw measles rash on her. An epidemic had commenced and now another quarantine. I nursed Jerry and Billy through the measles, spending hours reading to them in a shut-up bedroom. Ted escaped this time and Alice fled to grandma again.

When quarantine was lifted the kids got back to school, and Nan was able to shed her crutches and come home to live. Aunt Mary (Merriman) wanted to help her with her art ambitions and sent a teacher from high school to teach drawing and modelling in plaster. Of course the whole bunch of kids wanted to do modelling so the kitchen became a sculpture studio plastered with plaster. It required much scrubbing but they all had a wonderful time.

Meanwhile the father of the family kept up his hard and lonesome part, travelling back and forth to Oxford by team. He had a boarding place near Southford station, with a farmer's family, where he could keep Jenny, his horse. He spent Sunday there and several days to drive around and see people, then would take the train to Waterbury to come home for a few days. Grandpa gave him a little work to do, handwriting documents, which gave him a small addition to his meager

salary. The great desire of the Oxford parish was to find a
house where the minister could live. They had not had a
resident rector for years. In fact they were only a mission now,
receiving aid from the Missionary Society. They could only pay
a small amount raised by the parish and had to depend on
missionary help. This part of the salary came on time but the
parish part was always late.

Leading parish affairs in Oxford was Aunt Kate Davis. Aunt
Kitty, we called her, a most energetic old lady, lame and very
dear, but full of determination that the parish should have a
settled rector. She and Dad put their roseate ideas together
and were bound to cook up something. He drove around the
country many days, both in Oxford and Quaker Farms, looking
for a house large enough to hold his family. Quaker Farms
people wanted him to live over there, but Dad knew it would be
too hard entirely cut off from transportation. Oxford was bad
enough but it was only two miles from Tomantic R.R. station
and five miles from Seymour. The only transportation was by
horse and buggy.

Theo wanted me to come to Oxford for a Sunday and drive
around with him house hunting, so I went over one Saturday
and stayed two nights at his boarding house. The woman was
very nice and the church members were fond of the parson.

Her husband, a very crazy man, was well-educated but a
slave to the drink habit. I was so sorry for Mrs. Pierce that
Saturday night when her man drove in from his work hardly
able to stand up. He was much intoxicated. She fed him by
himself and tried to keep him away from us. He could not
unharness the horse and Mrs. Pierce got Dad to help her.
While they were out I tried to hide in the parlor and laid down
on the sofa. I did not want to see the drunken man, a new thing
in my experience.

He found my hiding place and stood over me as I lay on the
sofa. I trembled and kept quiet. He began waving his arms and

shouting about St. Pance, then looking fiercely at me said "I will give you black eyes." I meekly accepted that fact hoping he would not proceed to really give me black eyes. His wife came in and led him away and put him to bed. I heard him be sick in the night and raving.

The man always repented the next day and being a church member he knew his prayer book and we heard him saying the Litany. His wife said he always did that after being drunk.

Dad talked with the poor man and tried to get him to promise not to drink. I think he tried to reform but was sick soon after with some lung trouble and died not long after.

That Sunday Theo was to be at Quaker Farms, for morning service. I went with him. It was quite a drive over a high hill called the haystack, which separated the towns of Oxford and Quaker Farms. As we drove through the early spring country-side we passed a graveyard every few miles. I said to Theo, "There's nothing in this country but cemeteries." He replied cheerfully and tried to show me old farmhouses but it seemed to me just barren wilderness.

I liked the quaint old Quaker Farms church, although it was more of a meeting house than a church. No chancel, just a platform with altar set up. There were hard seats to sit on. I met some of the people and felt their critical eyes on me. We had dinner at the Walters' house and got a little acquainted with his family. They had nothing to suggest as to a rectory though they thought we ought to live there.

We drove back to Oxford for afternoon service. I met some of the people there. They were all friendly and I tried to be. It was a very old church, Gothic this time with a good chancel. Close to the chancel arch were illuminated the words, "In this place will I give peace." I thought to myself if I have peace there it will be the peace of a determined will, for I hate to come here. Nobody had any house to suggest so our drive back was heavy-hearted.

One happening during our life in the apartment I must tell. Dad was asked one evening to go to a parish social held in some far-out farmhouse. He got there before dark all right and tried to walk home with the flashlight. Although the people invited him to spend the night he started home. He soon lost his way. He tried to ask at a farmhouse but the dogs got after him as soon as he approached so he gave it up and just kept walking all night. At dawn he found himself at the Seymour RR station and found himself miles from Oxford. He took a train to Waterbury, came home and fell into bed. He slept for hours, then had a good meal and told us his adventures. I thought it was dreadful and wished he could live at home where I could guard him.

One day he came home radiant with joy and told me the parish had found a house for sale. Two hundred years old, fascinating but much out of repair but could be fixed up and made wonderful. The money to buy it had been raised by aunt Kitty and we could soon move over there. The family rejoiced together at the news of a house, though the girls were not in a hurry to live over there. From Dad's description I felt very dubious about getting into it for a long time but he had on his rosy glasses and would hear no objections.

It would be hard to express to you all I felt, when told so enthusiastically about this old house. I knew my dear man's propensity for looking through rose-colored glasses when intent on a project. I found that out when he persuaded me upon this missionary life in Connecticut which proved to be anything but rosy. Also I knew that he had a boon companion in aunt Kitty Davis, who was such an enthusiast for any project connected with the church, especially the Oxford parish. She loved the church there and felt the great need for a settled rector and a home for him to live in. She was a motherly soul, though childless herself, full of human kindness for everyone. She had a stout figure, not very tall, a large kindly face and a large stomach which she had a way of pressing against you when she talked confidentially. The girls soon got onto that and shied away from her.

It was largely due to her efforts that the really fine old house was at last put into shape for a rectory. I always thought there should be a tablet to her memory on the wall, but her name as well as Dad's is probably forgotten now in the Oxford parish. They were a quiet team and Aunt Kitty was mostly responsible for raising the $400 demanded to buy that old house.

Dad thought it a marvelous bargain and knew just what we needed to make it into a lovely home. I really tried to see it through his eyes when he took me to look at it, but while I thought the outside picturesque and a fine old antique, I could hardly picture the dilapidated interior being made into anything comfortable, unless perhaps tearing the whole thing down and building it over entirely. I asked who was going to pay for all the work and he said some of it would come from the Mission Society and Aunt Kitty and he would raise the rest.

I knew that by experience he could usually pull purse strings with his missionary talks so I ceased to worry about that. I had plenty to worry about after looking the house over in detail. It was a large gambrel-roofed structure, steep roof, rather small windows, no porch, a grass terrace in front of a stone path to the front door. It had never been painted and it was that nice old grey that Alice and Esther liked in old houses. It was said to be 200 years old and had been at one time an inn for travelers. There was an opening on one side with wooden shutters, which when pulled back revealed a window. We were told that in the old days liquor was passed out this way from the bar to the travelers in the stagecoach.

It was an interesting antique, but I shook my head mentally on the way home, seeing a forecast of what my life in that house would be. The plan was for us to move in as soon as the present inhabitants moved out, and live there while it was being made over. No rosy glasses could make me enjoy that prospect.

Theo thought it was necessary to move over at once so he could be on hand to watch the repairs, and the question was where could we live while the place was cleared out and the foundation timbers jacked up. They had rotted and had to be replaced. Aunt Kitty came to the rescue and said we could share her house, a white low-roofed little place right by a brook and with high hills towering over it and seeming very near. The whippoorwills shouted there at night and made me feel lonesome to think of living there.

Nan and Alice were to stay in Waterbury until we got settled as Alice was at St. Margaret's and Grandma was so good as to invite them to stay on. So Jerry and the boys and I prepared to move on. We began packing again and tearing up a home once more. The piano and heavy sideboard and enormous desk had to be taken out with block and tackle. The cellar was full of book boxes never unpacked, and of course I had to pack the china again and get everything ready to move. Then Dad took me and the three kids over and left us with Aunt Kitty, while he managed the move.

I was a homesick mortal that night going to bed in a damp room on the first floor, trying to unpack enough things to live with. The house was so near the brook in such a deep gorge under the hill that it was very damp. I remember my clothes used to feel almost wet in the morning. The children slept in a little loft up under the roof and thought it fun, as they always did when we moved.

When Dad got the furniture on the freight train he came and stayed with us. The family in the old house had not moved out yet and there was to be an auction. I must quote from old letters about that.

(This manuscript ends here. We have daughter Alice's narrative below to fill us in on the general way of life in Oxford. Unfortunately any descriptions of the day to day life of those three years, the kids' progress, and the times in the old house, are lost for now.)

Oxford Recollections
1902 – 1903

by Alice Marion Peck Snow

When my father, the Rev. Theodore Peck, became Rector in Oxford, in 1902, there was no rectory, so the family lived in a flat in Waterbury for the first winter, while Father boarded with a family in Southford.

There were five of us children, and my mother had a hard time as we had measles, chicken pox and whooping cough all in that one winter in those crowded quarters. Father held services on Sundays in Oxford and Quaker Farms, and spent part of the week making calls, driving his old horse Jenny from farm to farm. He had many adventures with this temperamental animal, for he was afflicted with night blindness, a disease which prevented the pupils of his eyes from enlarging as darkness came on, so that after dark he was completely blind.

If he had had a reliable and kindly dispositioned horse it would not have been too bad, but Jenny, we always said, was a devil in mare's clothing. Instead of bringing him home she would go into any barnyard hoping for oats.

When she stopped Father would get out and feel around to see if he could tell where he was. Sometimes unfriendly dogs would threaten to attack him. The owner of the house would come out to see what the racket was about and became suspicious when the poor parson would try to explain that he couldn't see after dark. On one occasion the horse stopped and wouldn't go on. On investigation he found out that they were on the edge of a pond. Jenny wanted a drink even if the parson didn't.

Finally, when spring came arrangements were made for us to board with a kindly woman known to all as Aunt Kitty Davis. She was a comfortable soul and let us pack into her tiny house under the hill.

My mother had a hard time that summer, cooking for so many on a hot wood stove in someone else's kitchen, with fat Aunt Kitty hovering about. Housekeeping was not easy in those days as there were no telephones, no cars, no deliveries except by the mailman. As local stores only carried groceries meat was ordered by mail and delivered the next day. If nobody was home he hung it on the mailbox. I remember one day when we were looking forward to steak, we came home to find that a ragged paper was all that was left of our steak. The dogs had gotten there first.

Meantime for a rectory the parish had purchased an old gambrel-roofed pre-revolutionary house. It had been a stagecoach tavern in ancient times. In the cellar was a great fireplace with crane and pots which had served many a hot toddy to weary travelers.

The building had also at some time served as a country store as evidenced by a ledger found in a walled-up closet in the chimney. This old document was an interesting record of barter exchange of produce for yards of dress material, calico and bombazine, potatoes for rum or molasses. I believe this book is preserved among the archives of the Diocese of Connecticut.

My Father being an antiquarian was thrilled with the old house, its romantic history and all these discoveries. He was an incurable optimist and could only see the place as it would be one day.

Not so with my mother. She saw only the stark reality of a filthy, run-down evil-smelling old house in a terrible disrepair.

The rooms downstairs were not too bad except for the dirt, but upstairs under the sloping roof most of the plaster had fallen down revealing rotting laths interspersed with the remains of squirrel and mice nests.

At last the slum family who had been living in the house moved out and some of the parishioners started to make repairs. By the time we had to move in the roof was unfinished and the carpenters refused to continue to work. They said it was too cold to be shingling a roof. Not only that but the underpinning of the house was open to the winds making it impossible to heat the house. Grandpa Abbott came over from Waterbury and spent a day stuffing leaves and hay into the foundation to keep out some of the cold.

There were coal stoves in the sitting room and dining room and a big oil range in the kitchen. Winters were severe in those days. The water in the well froze and Father had to break the ice before he could lower the bucket.

Plumbing was non-existent. We had outdoor facilities and an old washtub in the kitchen for Saturday night baths. Quilts were hung over lines forming a bath cubicle. Father drew the water from the well and Mother heated it on the stove. Then starting with the cleanest child the baths were one after the other, without changing the water.

Fortunately Nan and I were away at school so did not have to take part in these primitive ablutions.

Upstairs was like outdoors. Every night at bedtime saw a procession bearing hot soap stones and warm blankets up the stairs, the girls in one room and the boys across the hall. Everyone wore wool socks, sweaters, flannel nighties and caps.

Though the children throve, the poor Mother felt the strain of the back-breaking chores, and Father not only had to help with these but also manage two parishes, enduring the long slow drive to Quaker Farms Sunday afternoons after holding services in Oxford.

One time after a heavy rain on top of the snow an ice brook overflowed the narrow bridge. Jenny refused to go so the poor parson had to get out and lead her, getting thoroughly soaked himself. That trip nearly finished him for he did develop bronchial pneumonia.

Oxford was a very poor parish and had difficulty in raising the minister's salary. The collection went towards it. Another way the ladies tried to help was by holding cake socials. Everybody came and played games then ate ice cream and cake which they paid for. One time there was no money in the minister's house so he had to ask the ladies if he could charge the food until some money came in.

Sometimes donation parties were held to fill the parson's larder. On these occasions everybody brought contributions of flour, sugar, potatoes, vegetables and homemade cakes and pies, much of which were consumed at the party.

Part III

Settled Ministry –
Building a New Church, Washington, CT
1905-1920

(signed) Anna E. Peck 84 years old,
written in 1944 for the church history record

Rev. William Peck had charge of this parish for seven years
in combination with Marbledale. St. Andrew's had a rectory
and St. John's had none so he lived over there and held service
in one parish in the morning and the other in the afternoon,
arranging so that each parish had a morning service every
other Sunday.

My first view of St. John's was when I drove over with him
one Sunday after Christmas in the year 1881. Having become
engaged to his son, Theodore Peck, I spent some holidays
there. I remember the cold sleigh ride over Baldwin and
Church Hills, the snow-covered landscape, the little brown
church and a handful of people at the service. I little thought
that after twenty-five years I would be living here in the
rectory.

William Peck was a real missionary, visiting this whole
region, knowing who lived in every house. When the snow and
mud were so deep that he thought it not safe for horse and
buggy or sleigh, he pulled on his hip boots and tramped over
the hill to church or to visit the sick. He also held service in the
Romford schoolhouse, "when there was a moon," and I have
heard him give out in Marbledale church, "There will be a

service in Merryall schoolhouse at early candle-light." When we first came here to live there were people still living who remembered him and told us he baptized or married them.

After Mr. Peck came Charles Doupe, and then Dr. William Spencer. He came here with his widowed daughter Mrs. Cape, afterwards Mrs. Will Church, and her three children. They persuaded Miss Salome Morehouse to move out of her house, now the rectory, and let them rent it.

Dr. Spencer had private means as did Mrs. Cape and they made many improvements in the house, put in a furnace and bathroom, added a laundry and built a long, wide veranda on two sides of the house. Dr. Spencer was a scholar, had a large library, wrote fine sermons and did much good work. Mrs. Church was always an active worker and started many good endeavors in the parish.

Mrs. Orville Platt, wife of the Connecticut Senator, had built a house here and took a great interest in the work of the parish. She thought there should be a permanent home for the rector and offered to buy the house with the understanding that the women's Society of the parish would pay off the mortgage by 1897. Seventeen women signed this agreement and worked six years to pay off the mortgage. Soon after they began work they were saddened by the death of their rector, Dr. Spencer. This was in 1895. They kept on working and raised a good deal of money each year. They had ice cream and cake sales on the rectory lawn very week in summer, and one large sale at some private home each year. In winter they put on plays in the hall with local talent and gave turkey suppers. In 1901 the mortgage was paid off and the rectory became the property of the parish. It was placed in the hands of the Society for Donations and Bequests of the Diocese for safe keeping.

Of the seventeen women who undertook this great task, not one is living. Mrs. Church and Mrs. Mason who died last year were the last ones. The women's Society also made itself

responsible for the care of the rectory, repairs and improvements, and also some of the running expenses, insurance and
water rent. They kept on raising money with great success and
the most generous helpers were Mrs. Platt and Mrs. Van
Ingen. Dr. Spencer's life here gave the parish a good start and
Mrs. Church also did a great deal for it. Dr. Spencer is buried
in the cemetery near the church. His memorial is the stained-
glass window in the chapel given by his daughter and granddaughter.

Mr. Angell succeeded Dr. Spencer, and with his wife
enjoyed the rectory for two years. Although they were here so
short a time, Mr. and Mrs. Angell came very prominent in the
literary life of the town, as Mrs. Angell was secretary of the
women's Club for which she is said to have written very
entertaining minutes. At the same time Mr. Angell was
secretary of the Men's Club which was a flourishing concern in
those days. He wrote the history of the Club which is found in
the library; of his work as rector we find little record.

Then came Percy Robinson who preceded Mr. Theodore
Peck. He seems to have made rather an unsavory reputation
and we were told many tales of his misdoings. One seemed to
be that he was too much a sportsman and sometimes forgot a
weekday service when on the tennis court. He was a great
fisherman, as was also Rev. Robert Carter, pastor of the
Congregational Church. Dr. Henry van Dyke who spent the
summers here, wrote a rather fantastic tale describing the
rivalry of the two parsons in the catching of a giant trout. The
story, called "Leviathon," is published in the volume "Days
Off."

We were told that the Robinson children made themselves
very obnoxious to the neighbors and when in considering
calling Mr. Peck the committee were told that he had five
children, they said oh no, they couldn't have that. The Bishop
told them the Peck children were partly grown up and quite all

right. There were peculiar circumstances in the calling of Mr. Peck which may be interesting.

Bishop Brewster told us, chuckling, that the vestry men here did not seem ready to do anything about a change of rectors, but that three women came to Hartford to see him and begged him to remove Mr. Robinson and get them a new rector. He told them he could not send Mr. Robinson away with no place to go, he had a family and no money to move with. They said they would raise a sum of money (I think it was $400) to pay his moving expenses. After a while the Bishop found a place for Mr. Robinson in Bad Axe, Michigan, and then recommended Mr. Peck. The three women came over to Oxford one Sunday morning to hear Mr. Peck preach. We did not know who they were but very soon an invitation came for him to spend Sunday here and preach. This resulted in a parish meeting directly after church and Mr. Peck was called.

We moved here in Sept 1905 and Mr. Peck was told his first duty was to restore the reputation of St. John's Church which had suffered under Mr. Robinson.

Our family rejoiced at coming here after the discomforts of Oxford and thought the rectory quite a palace after living in an old house with wood stoves and no running water or other conveniences. Mr. Peck was so delighted with the place and the people and talked so enthusiastically to his clerical friends at the next Archdeaconry meeting that they laughingly said "Peck's found Paradise." It did seem like that after his ten years of missionary work in Eastern Connecticut.

The old church was an attractive building, well kept, lighted with oil lamps, heated by large stoves. It was cold underneath and we were told the Wykeham girls had to sit on their feet to keep them warm. We had no janitor and Daniel Knowles walked down from his place every Sunday morning to build the fires and ring the bell. He was a faithful church goer and Junior Warden. Miss Davies had started her school in

Blythe Hall on the village street and we had a small group of girls and a few boys from Gunnery. The vestry room was very cold and Mr. Peck had to shiver while preparing for service, which sometimes resulted in a croaking voice. After electricity came to town Miss Davies and the girls presented him with a small electric heater for the vestry room. Mrs. Van Ingen soon had electric lights put in the church and Mrs. Platt put them in the rectory. One more thing Bishop Brewster used to chuckle about was that long before women were allowed to vote at parish meetings in Connecticut they were doing it in Washington.

Later on Arthur Woodruff took the position of Senior Warden and Treasurer and kept it for twenty five years. I have often heard him tell how the rector came to his house and told him he *had* to be the treasurer of the parish. He said he did not want it and fought against it but Mr. Peck said he *had* to, so he did. He was always faithful to his duties and always at church, no matter how late he had been up Saturday night with his concerts here and in Litchfield. In winter he was in New York, very busy with giving music lessons, leading glee clubs and giving concerts, but he kept up his treasurer's work. The money was mailed to him and he kept the accounts and paid the bills. The parish has cause to be very grateful to Arthur Woodruff for his long years of service. I wish to put on record also the fine help the parish, rector and rectory family received from Miss Davies and the girls always filling some need or doing something nice for the church. It may interest the vestry to know that the parish had been paying $800 salary and Bishop Brewster told them he would not get them a rector at less than $1000. This was paid and afterwards raised to $1200. Mr. Peck and Rev. Robert Carter were good friends always and looked so much alike that one of the town humorists referred to them as "the heavenly twins." Both were getting bald, had brown beards, were about the same height

and swung their arms when they walked. There were no joint
services at that time except Hampton Sunday when all the
Protestant congregations gathered in the big church to hear
Dr. Turner, Chaplain of Hampton, and the quartette of negro
singers.

Mr. Peck had to sell his horse when he came here as there
was no barn or place to keep one so, while Mr. and Mrs. Carter
jogged comfortably around the country with horse and buggy,
Mr. Peck walked the parish, except that once a month he had
the loan of a carriage and pair of horses with driver, to make
distant calls.

On September 19, 1916 the Litchfield Archdeaconry met
here to celebrate the 100th Anniversary of the placing of St
John's Church on its present site. Historical addresses were
made, and a pamphlet for this anniversary was prepared for
this meeting through the efforts of Miss Davies and Mrs. Titus.
It contained photographs of the church and of Rev. Thomas
Davies and the Rector Mr. Peck, and extracts from the original
deed.

After a few years the old church began to seem too small.
City people were making their homes here, the schools were
growing larger, there was no place for the Sunday School and
we needed better heating arrangements. Mr. Peck made up his
mind to start a project for a new church and he wanted it to be
Gothic and of stone. He broached the subject to a group of
leading parishioners and was met by a decided refusal to
consider the subject. They said it would be impossible to raise
the money and he might as well forget it. Mr. Peck did not take
no for an answer and said he would lay aside the offerings at
early service and Saint days as the beginning of a fund. He
surprised the congregation the next Sunday by announcing
that he had started a fund for a new church and had sixty cents
in the treasury! He explained the reasons carefully and soon
the matter was taken up with enthusiasm. The ladies began

making plans for card parties and suppers to raise money, but Mr. Peck said no, he wanted it to be pure giving, and of course it would take a number of years. Two special offerings a year were taken and at those times the rector wrote many letters to people who had lived here or had reason to be interested in the church and the money began rolling in. Many large gifts were made and Mr. Peck was especially pleased with the moderate gifts of working people which meant real sacrifice. The Vestry wanted to take the Easter offering but the rector said no, we must keep that for missions.

When the fund had grown to good proportions Mr. Van Ingen became so interested that he said if they would get it to a certain point he would finish it. This gave an added impetus and soon plans were drawn and the cellar dug. Eric Rossiter was engaged as architect and gave the work his very best attention. He spent much time driving about the neighborhood selecting stone, buying up stone walls etc. The church was to be built of native stone of this region. Mr. Peck often went with him and they spent much time selecting just the right stone.

There were many delays owing to war conditions, and setbacks, such as springs bursting out in the cellar. As the work neared conclusion one of the finest things was the interest of the artists, Herbert Faulkner and H. Siddons Mowbray who gave their devoted services in the wood carving and paintings which were to beautify the church.

Mr. Van Ingen took the greatest interest in selecting the materials for finishing touches and the interior furnishings. Mrs. Van Ingen and Mrs. Platt and others were responsible for the beautiful altar hangings. These personal services made the church so much more valuable. There was an uncomfortable interlude the last winter of building. The builders wanted the chancel window as well as the stone steps and other things necessary to the new church, and this made the old building unusable. We did not know what to do, but it was finally decided to rent the lower hall, unsuitable though it was. There was no chancel of course, but the altar and lectern were moved down there and placed on the platform and a cabinet organ moved in. The brass cross and vases had been sent away to be re-lacquered and we had a wooden cross and glass vases. We managed to have our Christmas service under difficulties and got through Lent with one afternoon service a week, looking forward to Easter in the new building.

The corner stone had been laid in 1917 by Archdeacon Humphrey and the Masonic Lodge. The first service was on Easter Day 1918. The organ builder stayed up all night to finish the organ and played the service next day. It was a joyful and thankful day. Then the next month, May 1918, the church was consecrated by Bishop Brewster, and Dr. Chauncey Linsley preached the sermon. Many clergymen were here and there was a big dinner in the new parish room and many speeches.

There were no choir stalls as yet, or surpliced choir. The funds had all been used and Mr. Peck did not feel equal to raising any more money. That was left for Mr. Brown.

Mr. Peck was able to enjoy the fruits of his labors for two years and was obliged to resign in 1920 because of failing eyesight, having served the parish fifteen years. He left Washington for four years and then returned to spend his last days near his beloved church. He was made Rector emeritus by the Vestry. There is a memorial in the church to him and his father – the larger chalice and paten used in the Communion Service.

Epilogue
by Elizabeth Snow Rowe

Perhaps Anna stopped the "Chronicles" where she did because she was addressing only the early days of her marriage. When she finished, her children were old enough to have memories of their own of the subsequent years.

I wish she had continued the chronicles of her inner thoughts and reactions during the three years in Oxford and Quaker Farms. I hope the old house was livable when finally completed and that she had some good times during that period with her family. And she must have been excited and happy to be called to a settled parish in Washington, Connecticut, a small town with a parsonage where Theo's father had once been rector.

In a narrative written for the historical record of the church, Anna does describe their years in the rectory of St. John's from 1905 until 1920 when Theo retired due to blindness. After his retirement they then returned to their hometown of Waterbury for three years. In 1924 they moved in with widowed daughter Alice Peck Snow and her four children in "The Rooftree," across the street from the church in Washington, where they remained for the rest of their lives. Theo died in 1933, and Anna died in 1953 at the age of 93.

Alice's husband, Howard Birney Snow, a judge who raised money for Liberty Bonds during World War I, died of a brain hemorrhage in 1919 and left her a widow with four children under the age of six, one being my father who was two. Alice never remarried. Appendix II provides a narrative of life in the Rooftree in the 1930s, and was written by Marjorie's daughter Betty Lomele, who lived with Alice for a period as a teenager.

Betty in 1996 wrote this retrospective overview of Alice's life and times, up until her death in 1976 at the age of 89.

As a child I visited Grandma Alice in the Rooftree every summer, where we stayed overnight, and then accompanied her and other Snows to the summer place on an island in Bow Lake, New Hampshire, which was owned by her Uncle John Abbott (Anna's youngest brother). On one of these visits, Great Grandma Peck was still alive. I remember her as an elderly woman sitting in her rocker in the front parlor of the Rooftree.

When Alice was seventy, she sold the Rooftree and built her "dream house" on a nearby property. I visited often over the years. She spent most of her life caring for people, but did find time for watercolor and pastel paintings of the various New England landscapes. I have fond memories of those New Hampshire vacations with her and Uncle John, with skinny dipping, playing canasta by the light of a kerosene lamp, and going on painting outings with her a few of the highlights. Betty's description of Alice's adventuresome spirit resonates with my experience with her in her 60s and 70s.

The other four children had full and interesting lives. Marjorie died in her thirties, leaving behind at least one book of poetry. Her daughters, Betty and Dotty Wheeler, who lived with Alice as teenagers, are described in Appendix I. Nan had a career as a writer, illustrator and painter; her archives are housed in the Arizona Historical Society in Tucson, AZ.

Both sons of Anna and Theo served in WWI, as detailed in the Gunnery school archive. Ted went into business, married, and had three children. His granddaughter is the actress Mimi Rogers.

After serving in WWI, Bill was in the foreign service and served as a diplomat in many places. He worked in the consulate in Marseilles during WW II. Along with over one hundred American diplomats, he was held by the Nazis in Baden-Baden for five years.

Uncle Bill used to join us at Bow Lake, New Hampshire in the summer vacations in the 1950s. He was a quiet man who gave no hint of his multifaceted career. Uncle Ted lived in Arlington, VA when we lived there in the 1970s, and our little boys were thrilled with "Great Uncle Ted," by then a very elderly man.

Anna also wrote an essay about the Old Merriman House, included here in Appendix II. It describes Anna's visits to her grandparents during her childhood in the 1860s and gives a detailed description of farm life in rural Connecticut.

According to documents from Anna's youngest brother, John Vincent Abbott, a serious amateur genealogist, we are all descended from John Alden and Priscilla of the Mayflower, made famous by the 1814 poem by Henry Wadsworth Longfellow, *The Courtship of Miles Standish,* published nearly 200 years after their marriage in 1621.

Anna had ten grandchildren, and I don't have the count on the great grandchildren of my generation, and certainly not of my children's generation or their children's. I hope that this history makes its way to all her descendants, and that they find it interesting.

History has a way of repeating itself – whether because of nature, or nurture, or more likely a combination of the two. When John Alden landed at Plymouth Rock in 1620, I am sure he had no idea of what he started. But he must have known it would be something amazing.

Appendix I
The Rooftree
by Betty Wheeler Lomele
(daughter of Marjorie Peck)

Two things happened on my fourteenth birthday: I was
given a puppy, a black and white Cocker spaniel – love at first
sight – and I was told that my sister and I would be living with
our Aunt Alice Snow in Washington, Connecticut. Dotty, my
eleven-year-old sister, and I were quite used to being moved
around by now; we had just spent a year in a rather expensive
boarding school – probably too expensive for the Depression
years – and before that, three years in a much simpler farm
boarding school. Since our mother had died eight years earlier,
our life had been a combination of boarding schools, relatives,
and, for one brief year, a stepmother. So we looked forward
with great anticipation to this latest move to a life with an
actual family! We had spent quite a few Christmases with Aunt
Alice, my mother's older sister, our Peck grandparents, and the
four Snow cousins in their large, grey house called the Rooftree
in Washington, Connecticut.

Before getting acquainted with this family, I want to
describe the town and this house as I remember them.
Washington, CT was one of those post-card-perfect New
England small towns, complete with white-steepled church on
the village "green." Surrounding this green on three sides were
white colonial houses and the large, white Congregational
church on the fourth side. Streets radiated out – north, south,
east, and west – from the green, lined with more houses
behind white picket fences. All of this "older" town was on top
of a hill. The "lower," and newer town, known locally as the
"Depot" because that's where the train station was, meandered

along the foot of the hill and along the Shepaug river. All of the shopping was in the Depot, except for one lone combination soda fountain, convenience store and post office near the green up on the hill. The lower town was inhabited mostly by more recent immigrants: Germans, Czechs, Lithuanians, Swedes. You get the picture, I'm sure: a rather stratified social structure based on ethnic group and length of time in the New World. No one in either town could be called rich, with a few exceptions: there were a number of large estates where "old money" lived discreetly private lives.

Aunt Alice's house was about one block from the green but on the crest of the hill before it descended to the depot. Across the street from it was the only other church in the upper town: the Episcopal church. My grandfather Peck had been the rector of the church. In fact the rather impressive gray stone building had been erected on his watch. Halfway down the hill to the depot was the Catholic church – an appropriate place for it, my grandmother sniffed, as the congregation was mainly made up of "those immigrants" in the depot.

Our house, the Rooftree, was one of the large, shingled gray houses of indeterminate style – mostly Queen Anne, I think, but with many later additions. It had belonged to a doctor who had had his office on the first floor, just to the left of the front entrance hall. This was now my grandmother's room – a sunny sanctuary with many well-tended plants in the bay window looking east. I used to stop in there and visit with Grandma when I returned from school in the depot, warming myself on her floor register as I recounted the day's doings.

Straight ahead of the entrance hall was the dining room and to the right the living room – not a very large living room compared to the dining room and entrance hall. Perhaps it seemed smallish because it had so many entrances and exits and not much wall space: an archway opening to the dining room, the same to the hall, plus stairs going up and then a door to the front porch and another to the sun porch on the south side. Somehow, in the remaining space there was room for an upright piano, a fireplace, a long sofa, a rocker and bookcases, and last but not least, a hand-cranked phonograph.

On the other side of the large dining room, which also had a bay window with many plants, and through a swinging door, was a pantry and then the large, dark kitchen. Off the kitchen there was yet another after-thought of a room which housed the refrigerator and the washing machine – and Lord knows what else! Also, from the kitchen, stairs descended to the basement and up to the second floor – a narrow little "back" stairs leading up to what used to be the servants quarters in an earlier, more affluent age.

Back to the front hall: there, nice, wide stairs curved up to the second floor. Here were Aunt Alice's bedroom, and over the front porch a guest room, known, for good reason, as the ice box. It had windows on three sides – lovely in summer but icy in winter. My teen-age cousins Nancy and Jeanne had a large, sunny bedroom and next to it cousins Dick and Ted had an equally large room. Down the hall towards the back were three more bedrooms. The front room of these was rented out to a succession of boarders over the years and the back two bedrooms became mine and Dotty's.

But there's more: the front stairs continued to the attic where there was one large, unfinished room with dormer windows which was every child's dream of an attic to explore: trunks, boxes, old clothes, books, china, toys and on and on. The attic room I loved most was smaller. It had a dormer window looking to the west and down the valley and it was cousin Dick's own, private art studio – which I was invited to use! Dick was six years older than me and was just starting off to college. We had become great friends in the few weeks before he left, hiking in the woods, fishing and sketching. We both shared an interest in art of any kind. He introduced me to oil paints and, in fact, let me use any of his "stuff" that I wanted to. I accepted. I still have a portrait of my sister that I painted up in that attic room – my first attempt at portraits. Later that year Dotty and I constructed a puppet theater and puppets up there – well, at least a collection of dolls to which we attached strings – and we put on a puppet show for our obliging family.

This house was on a deep lot, perhaps half an acre. There was a garage with a chicken house, but no chickens. Behind it, a large expanse of lawn with several very large elm trees, hence the name "Rooftree." Then beyond the lawn, was a flower and vegetable garden (and source of worms for fishing) and beyond that an orchard of crab apple trees.

In all, a perfectly heavenly place.

Behind the Episcopal church across the street was the cemetery, rising farther up the hill. It was a pleasant and dreamy place of spring flowers and shrubs. My sister and I often took walks there – to us it was really not a melancholy place, even though our mother, who had been married in this church, was buried here. Shortly after we arrived to live with the Snows, my grandfather, old and blind by then, died and was buried there also. This gradually became a family plot and by now quite a few more Pecks and Snows are buried there.

Up on the green was a private boys' boarding school, The Gunnery, where Dick and Ted went to high school, and a little farther out of town was a girls' boarding school, Wykeham Rise. My mother had gone there, also my cousin Nancy, who was now in college, and eventually my sister went to high school there also. For elementary school, our family, and most others from the green, attended the public school down in the depot until high school and then – if money or scholarships were available – transferred to the private schools for high school. Since I was entering the eighth grade and Dotty, I think, the fifth, we naturally went downhill to the public school. I should point out that private schools in New England at that time were neither really "elitist" nor terribly expensive. They were just good schools, partly because private education in New England had a much longer tradition than public education, which came along about one hundred years later.

Dotty and I had no trouble adapting to the Snow household, which I'm sure was largely due to Aunt Alice, who soon became a "second mother" to us. A quite handsome rather than pretty woman, she was probably in her late 40s at that time. She had the distinguished aquiline nose of the Peck side of the family and wonderfully thick, curly brown hair that she wore in what seemed to me like a rather classical Greek statue style: a halo of curls around her face, kept tamed by a sort of band that formed a crown. All four Snow children also had this naturally curly hair. I dwell on this hair because I myself had nothing but straight, dish-water blond hair in a short, practical bob.

Aunt Alice was a non-nonsense, straightforward person with long experience, it seemed, in rising to any occasion, always "there" for family or friends. There ought to be one such person in every family who can always be counted on in any crisis, and in the Snow family Alice was it.

But she was so much more: fun loving, usually up for a spur of the moment picnic, a drive down to the Shepaug river to see what wild flowers were out, or just the fun of telling amusing stories about the goings-on around town as we took our turn drying the dinner dishes. I don't remember just how, but she got me started writing poems – really corny rhymes – about family doings.

Aunt Alice was the next to eldest of the five Peck children. Aunt Nan, a writer and illustrator of children's books was the eldest, then Alice, then my mother Jerry and, last but not least the two boys, Uncles Ted and Bill. Alice's husband Howard Snow, a young lawyer and judge, had died of a heart attack while making a speech to raise money for Liberty Bonds during World War I. Their youngest child, Jeanne, was only two at the time. Uncle Howard, fortunately, had left a small but sufficient estate to his widow – sufficient until the crash of the stock market in 1929. Not that the investments were all entirely lost but it became harder and harder, during the Depression, to keep the Rooftree afloat. Thus the "boarder" in the front room and a succession of student boarders who followed after Dotty and me – boys who came to Washington, CT to go to The Gunnery School. The year I lived there, I remember, Aunt Alice even developed a side business of baking homemade bread for the local inn.

So it had fallen to Alice to make a home for her parents. As time went on, after my grandfather died, it became harder and harder to take care of Grandma. She was quite overweight and suffered from arthritis, which meant a wheelchair and sponge baths and probably a lot more that I wasn't aware of. As she became increasingly bed-ridden it became harder and harder for Alice to lift her out of bed.

"Why can't you find a good woman to come in and help?" I can hear my grandmother asking querulously. "There ought to be some woman out there who would appreciate a good home."

But it wasn't easy to find one. For a year or so the town's visiting nurse boarded in the spare bedroom, and she was a great help as well as a good companion, but then she was transferred elsewhere. Aunt Nan would come for a period of time in the summer so Alice could take her brood off to New Hampshire for a vacation – a wonderful change. I'm sure she looked forward to those two weeks every year as much as the children did.

This rather negative view of my grandmother, as I saw her at fourteen, was completely revised – for the better – a few years ago when I acquired a long, unedited autobiography that she had written, probably in her 80s, based on her diaries. It was called "Chronicles of a Parson's Wife" and was absolutely fascinating: there she was, a young woman just setting out on married life, having babies, moving from one parish to another all over New England, all the trials and tribulations, highs and lows we have today but in such a different time and different setting. I'm so glad to have this memory of her to replace the rather gloomy one I had been carrying around all these years.

Much later in life and after Grandma, who lived into her 90s, had died, Aunt Alice was able to sell the Rooftree, since by then all her "chicks had flown the coop," as she would say. Two sisters from Waterbury bought the property with the intention of opening a funeral parlor. They apparently never got permission from the powers that be to operate a funeral parlor – on the Green – heaven forbid – but never-the-less they had it all renovated and painted and for a long time it just stood there, empty. Alice bought an adjoining acre or so of land behind the Rooftree with the same magnificent view down the valley and built the little cottage she had always dreamed of. She took up pastels and spent probably ten good years doing the things she had always wanted to do. She and an artist cousin, Ester Peck, would drive out to various sites in the area, set up their easels and record their love of nature in watercolor and pastel.

When Alice was in her 80s she flew out to California by herself to visit Al and me in San Luis Obispo. She was politely enthusiastic about California, but took a dim view of our tall, ungainly date palms lined up along the skyline: "scraggly poodle tails," she declared. The line of oil wells, dipping and rising rhythmically along the highway near Santa Maria reminded her of praying mantises. She was a woman of definite opinions which she didn't mind sharing.

A year or so later we saw her one more time. We were on a trip East and visited her in a nursing home near Washington,

Connecticut. Nobody had to "put" her there; she made the
decision herself in her practical way and seemed quite content
to be there. She died a few months later, peacefully listening to
music on the tape deck with earphones that had been a
Christmas present. My sister was by her side.

*(Note: As of August 2021, the Rooftree is still standing, at
75 Greenhill Rd, Washington, CT, and was recently sold after
being significantly restored to its original elegance.
According to Zillow, it was built in 1880.)*

Appendix II
The Old Merriman House
by Anna E. Abbott Peck

I feel moved to write my recollections of the old Merriman house which was built some year in the seventeen hundreds! We do not know just which one. It was bought by my great grandfather, Charles Merriman in 1815, and he went there to live when my grandfather, George Merriman, was four years of age. There is so little left now of Connecticut farm life that I feel like recording, for the benefit of the younger members of the family, the life that went on there in my childhood and youth.

It was one of the great Joys of my life to go to "Grandpa's House" for a visit, and the trip from Waterbury seemed quite a Journey, being made in the old days by horse and carriage. Later when the railroad was put through, what an adventure it was to go alone on the little train and climb up the steep Academy Hill to the green. Sometimes Grandpa and Grandma came down to Waterbury to bring the golden rolls of butter and dozens of eggs to our family and others, and took me back with them. Then I rode between them and watched Grandpa slap the reins and call out to his "colts", as he called them, Charley and Billy, high spirited old horses with thick tawny hides, almost orange color. We had to draw up at the big gate, always kept closed, for Grandpa to open it. Grandma would always remark, "Well, the old house is still here." I think she had a vision of blackened embers every time she ventured away.

I like to think how wide open and welcoming the house looked lying in the afternoon sunlight, with only the two great maples opposite the back door, the horse-chestnut in front, and a black cherry tree, which hung over the verandah roof and bore the most delicious fruit for us to climb after and eat. The original house must have been quite small, but Grandfather added the kitchen extension, the dormer windows and verandah, with their fancy trimmings. These were his great pride, but some of us think it was a pity to spoil the antique look of the house.

The wide front door opened into a large hall. On one side was the sacred best parlor, always shut up except on special occasions. It gave me a feeling of awe when I peeped in sometimes, as the blinds were closed and the room was dim, and I saw the black hair cloth chairs and sofa, set primly around the wall, the marble top table in the center, with a large Bible, and wax flowers under a glass globe. There was a "what-not" in the corner containing shells and curiosities, and the wall was hung with family portraits, and also a really fine copy of the Stuart portrait of George Washington and its companion, Martha. These were Grandpa's great pride. There was a fireplace and white wood mantel and some fine paneling and woodwork.

On the other side of the hall was the "sitting room", always open in summer. Here too was a fireplace and fine white woodwork. In winter a wood stove took the place of the open hearth. In this room was a beautiful mahogany sideboard, still envied by all the descendants, and used at that time only as a receptacle for books and pictures. Here too was the accordion with pearl keys which my mother played as a girl. Next to this room was the dining room, which was the real living room, and once the only kitchen as well, with huge fireplace and brick oven, long since disused. Grandmother's low, high-back chair stood in the chimney corner, and there was an old settle under the window, very hard, but with enough cushions that I liked to curl up there with my books.

I have pleasant memories of supper time in that big room, with the doors through the hall open, the evening sunshine slanting across the meadows, bird songs and the distant lowing of cows waiting to be milked, the plain clean tablecloth and thick dishes, the delectable rye bread and fresh butter, newly made cheese, thin shavings of pink dried beef, sometimes honey, cookies or crullers, and creamy milk to drink. Everything tasted so good, like the ambrosia of the gods.

It was a long busy day both indoors and out. I slept with Aunt Mary in the small bedroom off the sitting room. Early in the morning I would hear about four o'clock Grandpa's voice calling up the stairs to the farm boy, "Ho boy! Time to get up." Boy was sleepy and had to be called several times with increasing sternness. The men went off to feed and milk the cows, water the horses, then came in to breakfast and went right off again to the fields to hoe corn and potatoes and do all the work of raising the heavy crops of oats, rye and hay. It was a long hot morning, cheered by drinks from a stone jug containing a mixture of molasses, vinegar and water, kept cool under a shady hedge. Also there were great hunks of hard gingerbread, a delicacy I have never seen since those days, squares of toothsome ginger cake marked off with creases. It was hard enough to roll out but oh so good and soft to bite into.

Grandmother and Aunt Mary worked all morning too, washing for the "men folks," baking great loaves of rye bread, churning butter and making cheese. On the back porch was the old well with two oaken buckets, drawn up by a rope over a wheel, such delicious, sparkling water, never known to fail. Here they washed the clothes, drawing the water from the well, heating it on the stove and bringing it out again to the porch. I ate on the broad stone steps and conversed with them and when older gazed at the sky and dreamed my dreams or wrote poetry.

One of my favorite occupations was making the butter come. I turned the handle of the little red churn, and when the buttermilk that ran to the sides showed flecks of yellow, I peeped into the churn and saw the good smelling butter clinging to the paddles. Then Grandmother took it out and worked it with her hands and a small paddle until the milk was all out, and then molded it into beautiful golden rolls to be packed into jars.

I sat by Grandma and watched her turn a great cake of good smelling curd on to a board, and cut it into cubes, which when salted tasted very good. Then it was put between cheesecloths into a large round hoop and placed in the mysterious looking press. After several days of hard pressure it emerged as a delicious cake of "green cheese," almost white and tasting so good, we had some to eat and then it was put away to ripen.

Twelve o'clock brought the men home from the fields for dinner, and we sat down to a great piece of boiled salt pork, or home raised beef, whole potatoes and turnips, sometimes succotash or peas from the garden, finishing with apple pie and cheese. Sometimes Grandpa went down cellar and brought up a pitcher of hard cider, which some of the family thought helped to cause his rheumatism.

Back again to the fields while the women washed dishes, scaled milk pans and finished the cleaning and ironing, then sat down for a little respite in midafternoon, having washed and combed and put on clean calico dresses. Grandma sat in her high back chair and sewed sheets or mended socks or some such homely task, while resting her muscles from hard labor. Perhaps it was this habit of midday rest that helped her to live more than ninety years. At five o'clock work began again, feeding chickens, taking care of the milk, etc. I loved to help feed the chickens and collect the eggs in the low hen house. I would shell the corn and put some on my shoe and it was fun to feel their sharp beaks pecking it. They got so tame they would eat out of my hand and Aunt Mary could pick up a hen and rock it to sleep in her arms while singing to it. I never attained to that but could sometimes pick one up.

On rainy days the kitchen chamber was a fine place to stay.

There were old spinning wheels to play factory with; the old wooden cradle that my mother was rocked in, now used by the cat as a hiding place for her babies. There was a chimney closet, dark and smelly, where hams were smoked, and many corners to explore.

The Sundays have a special memory shelf in my mind, and I often recall them in these hectic days, when it is hard to get any quiet, what with the rush of automobiles, the hurrying about, the picnics and Sunday journeys. Breakfast was later and there was the unusual treat of "butcher's meat," a steak broiled over the coals of a wood fire, oh, such a flavor! Fried potatoes with platter gravy, pancakes, those delicious concoctions never eaten by me anywhere else, made of flour and cornmeal, raised overnight, thick and mossy, and eaten with thick cream, sweetened. Would that I might taste them again. Delicious coffee too and time to eat a more leisurely meal. Then I had the pleasure of watching Grandpa shave. It was quite a ceremony. He got all his tools together on the table before the looking glass in the living room, covered his cheeks and chin with lather, and then applied the razor slowly and carefully, drawing down his mouth in funny grimaces. I watched the process, fascinated.

Then he brushed his Sunday coat and had to be helped into it, as he had lame shoulders. Grandma and Aunt Mary finished their work and got into their best dresses, kept in one closet in the front hall. Their whole wardrobe was not too large for that one closet. My best hat, trimmed with white ribbon and pink roses, was taken out of a drawer in the big sideboard in the hall. It always smelt of wine, for in the cupboard of the sideboard were kept the bottles of grape and blackberry wine which Grandma made herself and which she indignantly denied had any alcohol in. "Why, I didn't put a drop in it, it's just juice." But it was deliciously fermented juice.

One of the country customs now gone by was the ringing of the nine o'clock bell, as a warning that church time drew near, and a guide for setting the family clocks. I can still recall the sound of those country bells pealing out on the still air, and the sensation of peace and quiet as I sat on the steps waiting for it to be time to go to church. There seemed to be a restful hush over the sunny meadows, and the bird songs had a peculiar sweetness. The Episcopal bell had a deep tone and blended harmoniously with the lighter key of the Methodist and Congregational bells as they rang out each in their turn. Grandpa usually started for church first, then Aunt Mary and I, and Grandma last, hurrying across the green to get there before the bell stopped tolling. Aunt Nancy Holcomb joined the procession too and we all sat in the two front seats.

How distinctly I remember the service in the Old Christ Church. It was my first acquaintance with the Episcopal service, as my mother after her marriage went to the Methodist with my father and we were brought up there. I loved the pealing out of the organ from the back gallery where the choir sat, and I learned to find the places in the prayer-book. Those red-faced farmers knew how to read the psalter and their voices rang out in the responses. We had the full service in those days, Morning Prayer Litany, commandments and all. I can still hear Grandma and Aunt Nancy in the responses to the Litany and "Lord have mercy upon us" after the commandments. Aunt Nancy had artificial teeth and one Sunday she lost them out during the prayers and I had to crawl under the seat to find them. Before the sermon, white haired Dr. Lewis would go into the vestry room and change his white surplice for a black gown. It was not thought proper to preach in a surplice. I used to watch for his head to appear as he climbed the stairs at the back of the high pulpit. During the sermon I studied the designs in the great east window, so rich in color, the Good Shepherd in the center, and small ecclesiastical design at the sides. I wondered what they meant, the pelican, the lamb bearing a cross, the wheat and grapes and symbolic figures. I stayed to Sunday School with Aunt Mary, who taught a class.

Then we hurried home to have a cold lunch of doughnuts, pie and milk before the afternoon service, which the farmers insisted on having, sermon and all, but during which some of them slumbered and snored peacefully. Later on, a modern minister persuaded them it was better to have the second service in the evening. After this was a quiet space, when Grandpa and Grandma sat in their high back rockers in the sitting room and dozed peacefully over the Sunday papers. Aunt Mary and I sometimes went to the woods or sat on the porch with our books. Supper was early and we had a hot dish, ham and eggs or clam stew. Then the chores and early to bed to get up refreshed for another week's work. What a contrast to the modern Sundays! These faithful Church people, in spite of hard labors, never missed a service.

Sometimes in my older girlhood I went up there in the Christmas holidays and had a chance to see something of winter life in the country. There was the excitement of pig killing, the tying out of lard and grinding of sausage meat, and seeing the hams and bacons put in the chimney to smoke. There was plenty of outdoor work with wood cutting and hauling, care of horses and cattle, but there was more leisure than in summer. My grandfather read a great deal, especially in the evening, sitting in his wooden armchair with a candle in his hand, held so close to the book or paper that I expected to see it burst into flames, especially when he nodded and fell asleep. He read large volumes of American history, biography and travel, and one winter made a pilgrimage to Washington, DC, to see a Presidential Inauguration, a great event in his life.

In these winter visits I slept upstairs in the big four poster bed, and thought it fun to jump into the feather bed and snuggle down under the thick quilts. I had a tallow candle for light and loved to blow it out and then smell it as its little red eye faded away. How those scents linger in the memory! Quilting was

done too in those winter days. I made my wedding quilts up
there, with Grandma's help, before I was married.

One distinct feature of the winter life was family prayers.
There was no time in summer. This was a unique ceremony,
never seen by me anywhere else. Grandma sat in her high back
chair with the large family Bible on her lap, and read a long
chapter, usually from the Old Testament, and how well she
read, slowly and distinctly. Then Grandpa would get up from
his wooden armchair, go to the bedroom and get his prayer
book, step out on the back porch and clear his throat with much
hemming and hawking, then stand in front of his chair while he
found his place, knelt down, and read the prayers from a family
prayer book. I was inclined to laugh during that long interval,
and Grandma sometimes carried on conversation. I always
wondered why he did not get his book ready before she began to
read, but he always followed the ceremony. Once when I was
engaged and had my lover there with me, Grandma read the
story of Jacob serving fourteen years for Rachel, and Grandpa
kept his eyes fixed on me with such a funny twinkle that I felt
quite embarrassed.

During my romantic days I loved that place above all others
and often went there to dream my dreams and confide my
secrets to my beloved Auntie, who never failed to sympathize.
She was intensely interested in young love affairs and I'm sure
she longed sometimes for a larger life herself, and a chance to go
out and travel and develop her wide-awake mind in many ways,
but it was the accepted tradition of those days that the last
daughter should stay with the old folks and so she gave up her
desires and stayed faithfully on. She nursed her mother through
double pneumonia when over ninety years of age, and saw them
both through the feebleness and illnesses of old age to the end.

~~O~~

ABOUT THE AUTHORS

ANNA ELIZABETH ABBOTT PECK, daughter of businessman Ansel Abbott and Nancy Merriman Abbott, was born in 1860 in Waterbury, CT. She married Theodore Mount Peck (1857-1933) in 1883, after three years of engagement. She grew up in a large well-educated family and attended St Margaret's Academy in Waterbury. Her father, Ansel, also wrote a family history, which survives as an impeccably handwritten notebook, now part of the family archives. Anna died in 1955 at age 95.

ALICE MARION PECK SNOW (1886-1976), Anna's second child, attended Smith College and then married lawyer and judge Howard B. Snow. Howard died at age 39, leaving Alice with four children under the age of six. She reared these children, and housed them, as well as various relatives, in the Rooftree, a large Victorian house across the street from St John's Episcopal Church in Washington, CT. Her father had built the church during his tenure there, as described in these *Chronicles*. Anna and Reverend Peck lived with Alice in their later years, when Alice helped Anna assemble the *Chronicles*.

ELIZABETH (BETTY) WHEELER LOMELE was the elder daughter of Marjorie Ruth Peck Wheeler, Anna's third child. Marjorie died in her 30s, and daughters Betty and Dorothy Wheeler lived with Alice in the Rooftree for several years, as teenagers, along with Alice's four children and various other relatives. In this volume, Betty writes in 1997 of this house and her childhood experience there as well as some of the subsequent history of the family and household.

ELIZABETH SNOW ROWE is daughter of Alice's third child, Theodore. She earned a Ph.D. in biochemistry from Duke, and has had a successful career in scientific and medical research, pharmaceutical development, and writing. She is the author of *Sailing Downwind: Poetry and Stories*. Elizabeth is also a sailor, painter, sculptor, pilot, horsewoman, and avid reader. She and husband Vernon D. Rowe live in Shawnee, Kansas, and Santa Monica, California, near their two sons and five grandchildren.